Cultural
Amnesia

CULTURAL
AMNESIA

AMERICA'S FUTURE AND THE CRISIS OF MEMORY

STEPHEN BERTMAN

PRAEGER

Westport, Connecticut
London

Library of Congress Cataloging-in-Publication Data

Bertman, Stephen.
    Cultural amnesia : America's future and the crisis of memory /
    Stephen Bertman.
        p.   cm.
    Includes bibliographical references and index.
    ISBN 0–275–96230–X (alk. paper)
    1. Memory—Social aspects—United States.   2. Academic
    achievement—United States.   3. Democracy—United States.   4. United
    States—Social conditions—1980–   5. United States—Intellectual life—
    20th century.   6. Culture.   7. Literacy—United States.   I. Title.
    HN59.2.B474   2000
    306'.0973—dc21   99–43113

British Library Cataloguing in Publication Data is available.

Library of Congress Catalog Card Number: 99–43113
ISBN: 0–275–96230–X

First published in 2000

Praeger Publishers, 88 Post Road West, Westport, CT 06881
An imprint of Greenwood Publishing Group, Inc.

Printed in the United States of America

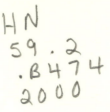

The paper used in this book complies with the
Permanent Paper Standard issued by the National
Information Standards Organization (Z39.48–1984).

10 9 8 7 6 5 4 3 2 1

For Brandon and Logan,
whose memories
are just beginning.

History is to the nation . . . as memory is to the individual. An individual deprived of memory becomes disoriented and lost, not knowing where he has been or where he is going, so a nation denied a conception of its past will be disabled in dealing with its present and its future.

Arthur M. Schlesinger Jr.
The Disuniting of America

CONTENTS

ACKNOWLEDGMENTS

Acknowledgments are the expressed memory of the debt we owe to others. Such a section is especially appropriate in a book whose subject is memory itself.

I therefore wish to thank the following individuals who have helped to make this book a reality by sharing their time and thoughts with me: Charlotte Crabtree, Tony Harrigan, Donald Hayes, Philip J. Hilts, Gertrude Himmelfarb, E.D. Hirsch Jr., John Kotre, Rita Kramer, Bruno V. Manno, Gary B. Nash, Diane Ravitch, Daniel L. Schacter, Arthur Schlesinger Jr., Gilbert Sewall, Patricia Weiss, Max Weismann, and Susan Wendt-Hildebrandt.

Thanks are also due to my literary agent, Ed Knappman, and my publisher for their commitment to this project, and to my secretary, Margie Prytulak, for her diligence and labor in preparing the manuscript for publication.

I also owe a special debt to my wife, Elaine, for the memories we share and for her inspiring faith in the power of education.

THE LAND OF THE LOTUS-EATERS

The Odyssey of Homer is one of humanity's oldest stories. For most people it is a tale of adventure, one that describes the exploits of a seafaring Greek hero named Ulysses.[1] Yet of the book's twenty-four chapters, only eight deal with maritime adventure. The rest of the story, two-thirds of it in fact, takes place in Greece, Ulysses' homeland. For in reality *The Odyssey*'s principal theme is not the exploration of the exotic but the restoration of the familiar, not the investigation of alien lands but the moral reconstruction of domestic society.

In this story, memory plays a key role. When the hero's adventures are described, they are presented as a series of recollections: near the end of his voyage, Ulysses recounts to his audience—and to us—his memories of all that happened in the ten years since the Trojan War ended and he set sail for home.

In the adventures themselves, the theme of memory continues to play a role. Soon after leaving Troy, Ulysses and his men come to a land where a curious plant, known as the lotus, grows. After his scouts fail to return, Ulysses goes in search of his men and finds them sitting with the natives, feasting on the lotus's sweet fruit.

Whoever ate the lotus's honey-sweet fruit wished neither to report back nor return, but longed to stay there, feeding on the lotus with the natives, oblivious to home. I had to use force to bring them back to their ships, and they cried all the way. After dragging them in, I tied them under the rowing-benches. Then I ordered the rest of my trusty crew to board the swift ships quickly before anyone else tasted the lotus and forgot about home.[2]

Stripped of remembrance—the poet implies—we can never find home, for we will have ceased to know its location and its claim upon our lives.

Ten years later, alone now and shipwrecked, our hero is washed ashore on another land, a lush island in the middle of the sea inhabited by a sensuous goddess named Calypso.

A big fire blazed on the hearth, and the smell of split cedar and juniper floated over the island. She was singing inside with a lovely voice, plying her loom with a golden shuttle as she wove. Outside, around the cave, spread a wood thick with alder and poplar and fragrant cypress, and in it long-winged birds perched at rest—owls and falcons and sharp-tongued cormorants that labor at sea. Around the cave's mouth ran a thick vine laden with clusters of grapes, while nearby sparkling water sprang—now this way, now that—from a row of four fountains. Beyond lay a soft meadow where violets and parsley grew. There even a god, had he visited the place, would have marveled and rejoiced in his heart.[3]

Lonely and passionate, the goddess Calypso welcomes Ulysses and falls in love with him. She offers him the gift of immortality if only he will stay with her forever. But Ulysses resists, for he longs for something else. We see him "sitting on the shore, his eyes ever wet as his sweet life ebbed away,"[4] staring out toward the far horizon beyond which lay Ithaca, his home. To accept Calypso's offer would mean to renounce that home and those who need him there—his wife, his young son, and the people who looked to him as their leader. Staying with Calypso would mean severing every tie that made him who he was.

It is no accident that the poet calls Ulysses' temptress "Calypso," for it is a name that in ancient Greek means "the hider." By keeping Ulysses on her remote island, Calypso would be hiding him from the world; but she would also be hiding him from himself, from the self he was and the self he could someday become, sustained and guided by the memory of those he loved.

Prompted by the Olympian gods, Calypso eventually yields to their will and allows Ulysses to sail for home. But his homecoming is not without struggle. Once back in Ithaca, he must challenge and overthrow a cabal of arrogant young nobles who have camped out in his palace in order to claim his wife and throne. These nobles had grown up during the twenty years Ulysses had been away (ten at Troy and ten at sea), years when Ithaca had no king to preserve moral order. The nobles had forgotten the very meaning of morality. Ulysses had come home to remind them. Just as the first quarter of *The Odyssey* delineates the moral degradation of Ithaca, so will the poem's last half describe its moral reformation.

This concern with social reconstruction reflects the times in which *The Odyssey* was composed. The poem evolved not during a glorious age of grandeur, but a dark era of economic and political chaos following the collapse of Greece's heroic age. The palaces were in ruins, the royal families dead or in exile, all arts save pottery forgotten. Dialectal clues and other internal evidence suggest that *The Odyssey* wasn't even composed in Greece but on the western shores of Turkey where refugees had fled to begin life anew. The Greeks of the Dark Ages nostalgically longed for a world that was lost, for a spiritual and psychological home kept alive only in remembrance and imagination. It was this vision of how life once was and how it could be again that sustained their faith, a vision articulated in the architectural symmetry and rhythmical harmony of Homeric verse.[5] To the ancients who heard his tale, Ulysses was an inspiration and source of hope. Through recollection and determination, his tale told them, the scattered fragments of a shattered world could be found and mended once again into wholeness.

A FORGOTTEN *ODYSSEY*

Today, in most people's minds, Ulysses and *The Odyssey*—Homer's *The Odyssey*—have ceased to exist.[6] Nor are these the only things from the past our society has forgotten. For reasons that this book will make clear, "cultural amnesia," the loss of cultural memory, is one of the most telling symptoms of America's current state of mind. Each day, fewer and fewer of our nation's long-term memories survive; each day, our country's short-term memory grows ever shorter.

According to Gallup polls, 60 percent of adult Americans don't know the name of the president who ordered the dropping of the first atomic bomb.[7] Among college seniors, 42 percent can't place the Civil War in the right half century, and 24 percent think Columbus discovered America in the 1500s.[8]

This "dumbing of America" cannot be viewed simplistically as the short-term loss of social studies trivia. Instead, it must be recognized as the loss of a longer-term set of historical memories without which no civilization can prosper or long endure. Just as an individual needs memories to maintain a sense of personal identity, so a nation needs them in order to survive.[9]

Cultural Amnesia addresses this issue, combining psychological insights into the nature of memory with perspectives on the meaning of democracy and its prospects. It argues that cultural amnesia, like Alzheimer's disease, is an insidiously progressive and destructive illness that is eating away at America's soul. Rather than superficially blaming national memory loss on a failed educational system, the book looks beyond the schoolroom to the larger forces that conspire to alienate Americans from their past: a materialistic creed that celebrates transience, and an electronic faith that worships the present to the exclusion of all other dimensions of time. Indeed, it is these forces, more than any others, that will govern the course of American history in the twenty-first century.

CHAPTER 1

CULTURAL AMNESIA

Each of us has our odysseys. Three years ago, my wife—convulsed by violent seizures and unconscious—was taken to emergency by ambulance. She had suffered a severe withdrawal reaction to a dangerous prescription drug.

In the middle of the night as I sat by her hospital bed, she awakened and asked me what had happened. I told her in great detail. She reached out her hand to mine and said, "I love you," closed her eyes and slept.

The next morning she awoke and asked me what had happened to her. I explained again in the same detail, realizing this time that she had forgotten everything I had told her the night before.

It was not the last time she would ask, nor the last time I would answer. Like a magnetic tape erased by an electrical charge, my wife's short-term memory had been wiped clean by the seizures that had sent bursts of neural energy surging through her brain.

For days she did not know what year it was or the name of the current president of the United States. After she left the hospital, we learned that there would be much more that she did not recall or would ever remember. Events that had occurred, intimate experiences that had been shared, places that had been visited in the weeks and even months before the attack were simply gone as though they had never happened. With repeated association and by patient effort, some memories returned. Others are irrevocably lost. Life goes on.

Through it all, I still remember her hand reaching out to me in the darkness, remember her saying, "I love you," knowing who I was, knowing who *we* were, despite all that had been suffered.

My wife's perseverance in recapturing her life has taught me how much of what we call our personal identity is really the sum total of our memories. In many ways it is our memories that tell us who we are. Interlinked, they form a chain of continuity from the past to the present that helps us keep our bearings as we journey through life. We save photographs of birthdays and weddings, old letters and greeting cards, souvenirs of trips taken, not because we are pack rats but because we are human. Indeed, to be human *is* to remember.

Could it be that what is true for an individual is also true for a society? If memories are essential to our sense of personal identity, might they also be essential to our sense of identity as a nation? Indeed, can a culture deprived of memory go on? And if national memory loss implies a loss of direction, what will be the consequences for our future as a people and as a civilization? Indeed, can any culture have a viable future if it has lost touch with its past?

DIAGNOSTIC QUESTIONS

Should a patient exhibit symptoms of confusion and disorientation, a doctor may ask a few standard questions: Do you know where you are? Do you know what day it is? Do you remember what happened before you got here? Do you remember your name? Such questions, when asked of Americans at large, offer disturbing evidence of amnesia on a national scale.

"Do you know where you are?" In 1988 the National Geographic Society commissioned the Gallup Organization to conduct an international survey to measure how well Americans know geography.[1] The survey queried more than ten thousand adults in nine industrialized nations: the United States, Canada, Mexico, the United Kingdom, France, West Germany, Italy, Sweden, and Japan. As part of its investigation, the survey questioned young adults between the ages of eighteen and twenty-four, the most recent products of their countries' educational systems. Subjects were shown an unmarked map of the world and were asked to locate the countries named above as well as the Soviet Union, Egypt, South Africa, Vietnam, Central America, the Persian Gulf, and the Pacific Ocean. In addition, they were asked other questions about geography.

In the international competition, the American team came in dead last. Two out of three American adults couldn't find Vietnam; three out of four couldn't find the Persian Gulf; almost half didn't know where Central America was located; 15 percent put South Korea in the north and North Korea in the south; 43 percent couldn't find England on a map of Europe; and 14 percent couldn't even find the United States on a map of the world.

Among the eighteen-to-twenty-four-year-olds tested, young Americans scored the worst of any nation, identifying only 6.9 out of sixteen possible locations. The United States, moreover, was the only country in which its most recently educated citizens performed more poorly than its oldest.

Local surveys reinforced the results of the international one.[2] Forty percent of high school seniors in Kansas City couldn't name three South American countries. Thirty-nine percent of high school seniors in Boston couldn't name the New England states.

In the late 1940s, the Gallup Poll had conducted "Geography Derbies" similar to the survey it ran in 1988.[3] In fact, the 1988 survey used exact reproductions of the very maps that had been employed forty years before. Back in 1947, American adults with some high school education were able to identify the locations of six out of twelve European countries.[4] By 1988, high school *graduates* could identify only 3.4.[5] Ironically, 57 percent of the adults polled in 1988 confidently asserted they knew more about geography than did their parents' generation.[6]

Gilbert M. Grosvenor, president of the National Geographic Society, summed up the disheartening results of the survey. "Have you heard of the lost generation?" he asked. "We have found them. They *are* lost. They haven't the faintest idea where they are."[7] Commented Grosvenor: "Our adult population, especially our young adults, do not understand the world at a time in our history when we face a critical economic need to understand foreign consumers, markets, customs, foreign strengths and weaknesses. . . . [8] The world is too competitive and dangerous to be a vague blur of memorized names and places. Without geography, we're nowhere."[9] "If remedial steps are not taken," cautioned the report, "this generation of Americans may pass down their geographic ignorance to the next."[10]

Indeed, converting the results of such surveys into percentages may actually mask the true extent of our lostness.[11] If 14 percent of Americans couldn't find the United States on a map, we might take comfort in the fact that 86 percent *could.* But in flesh-and-blood terms, that means there were twenty-four million Americans who couldn't find America. Just as there were forty-four million who couldn't point out the Pacific Ocean on a map—even though, if they had been blindfolded, they'd have had almost a fifty–fifty chance of getting it right since the Pacific covers 46 percent of the globe.[12] In fact, in flesh-and-blood terms, fifty-eight million Americans couldn't tell east from west.

According to a report sent to Congress in 1998 by the National Science Foundation, ignorance like this can be of cosmic proportions. According to the NSF's survey, "only 48 per cent of Americans know that the earth goes around the sun once a year."[13]

Can a democracy survive in an increasingly global society when so many of its citizens are so "spaced out"? Perhaps it's time to try another question or two in our national memory test.

"Do you know what day it is? Do you remember what happened before you got here?" In 1986, a Department of Education survey, the National Assessment of Educational Progress, tested eight thousand typical seventeen-year-olds on their knowledge of history.[14] Their answers fell wide of the mark. Many missed even when asked to pick the right fifty-year period when a certain event had taken place. One out of three high schoolers didn't know in what half-century the Declaration of Independence had been written, and three out of four couldn't locate the presidency of Abraham Lincoln. One in five thought the radio and telephone had been invented after 1950.

Three years later, the National Endowment for the Humanities commissioned the Gallup Organization to question seniors in college about their knowledge of history.[15] As it turned out, 25 percent thought Columbus landed in America after 1500; 60 percent didn't know the "shot heard round the world" was fired at Concord, Massachusetts; and 23 percent thought "from each according to his ability, to each according to his need" came from the U.S. Constitution rather than from the writings of Karl Marx. If this poll of seven-hundred college seniors had been a history test with a passing grade of 60, more than half the students would have failed.[16]

By 1994, the year that marked the fiftieth anniversary of the Normandy invasion, fewer than half the American adults who were polled remembered that Dwight Eisenhower had been the Allied Forces' Supreme Commander.[17] CBS News also found out that 22 percent didn't even know who America's enemies had been in World War II.[18]

Almost fifty years after the first atomic bomb dropped on Japan, many Americans were unsure such a device had ever been used in war. In a 1995 "America's Talking" Gallup poll,[19] 22 percent of those surveyed did not know where—or even if—an atom bomb had been dropped. Sixty percent did not know the name of the president who gave the order: 2 percent thought it was John Kennedy; 1 percent, Richard Nixon.

In a 1996 survey of five hundred seniors graduating from Florida's top universities,[20] only about one in ten knew Lyndon Johnson originated "the Great Society."

A survey sponsored by Congress also found that of American high school seniors fewer than half knew that containing Communism was the primary goal of U.S. foreign policy from 1945 to 1990.[21]

In another poll—a survey of students attending Harvard, Yale, Princeton, Brown, Dartmouth, and the University of Pennsylvania[22]—40 percent of those questioned couldn't name Britain's current prime minister, 20 percent couldn't name a single sitting Supreme Court justice, and half couldn't name the two senators then representing their home state.[23] Their ignorance may have implications not only for their future capability as citizens but also for the future competence of American government and business: at the time of the survey, 38 percent of all U.S. senators, 25 percent of all members of the House, and 40 percent of all corporate CEO's had come from just such Ivy League schools.[24]

Over the years, Benjamin J. Stein conducted focus groups drawing upon students from Los Angeles high schools and universities.[25] In his work Stein encountered a widespread ignorance of geographical and historical facts combined with a widespread ignorance of concepts and concluded the two are connected. Said Stein: "The kids I saw (and there may be lots of others who are different) are not mentally prepared to continue the society because they basically do not understand the society well enough to value it."[26]

According to a 1998 *New York Times* article, "More American teen-agers can name the Three Stooges than the three branches of the Federal Government."[27]

But such a problem can also be traced to those who are younger. In an earlier survey of eight-to-twelve-year-olds, *Washington Monthly* found that "they could name 5.2 alcoholic beverages but only 4.8 presidents."[28]

A case of amnesia can be identified by probing a patient's awareness of the framework of space and time within which his life is lived. "Do you know where you are?" the physician asks. "Do you know what day it is?" In similar fashion, cultural amnesia can be diagnosed by examining the mind of a nation, by testing its understanding of geographical and historical realities, the spatial and temporal parameters of its activities and existence. If, as individuals, we do not know where we are or what time it is, we are lost. If, as citizens and as a country, we are ignorant of geography and history, our national future is in peril. Unmoored from both space and time, we float in zero gravity, intellectually adrift.

"*Do you remember your name?*" Of course, our identity is based on more than just knowing where we are or what time it is. Even denied this information, a victim of kidnapping, awakening from unconsciousness in a dark cell, still knows who he is. For his sense of identity is drawn from a wider and deeper reservoir, the reservoir of personal experience and knowledge. Yet there is evidence that this reservoir too is drying up for us as a nation, not because of a drought of information, but because we are losing our capacity to drink.

In 1992, the National Assessment of Educational Progress tested the literacy of twenty-six thousand adult Americans.[29] Extrapolating from its findings, the Department of Education concluded that half of all adult citizens—some 95 million of us—lacked the basic skills required to compose and comprehend written English: the ability, for example, to write a letter complaining about a billing error or to understand written instructions intended for prospective jurors.[30] Weaknesses in literacy were matched by comparable weaknesses in numeracy: only 52 percent of those surveyed could figure out the length of a bus trip using a printed schedule; only 4 percent could compute the interest they would pay for a loan.[31] Sadly, the group that later scored the lowest in literacy had earlier shown the highest confidence in its own abilities: seven out of ten had declared they could read and write English well or even very well.[32]

In another 1992 national study, a study focusing on numeracy,[33] 70 percent of fourth graders were found incapable of doing third-grade math, 80 percent of eighth graders were found unable to do seventh-grade math, and 94 percent of high school seniors were found unprepared for mathematics on a college level.[34] Questioned earlier, however, 68 percent had confidently asserted they were "good at math."[35]

When the 1994 results of the National Assessment of Educational Progress were released, progress *isn't* what they showed. The results revealed students were learning less than they had been in 1992, especially high school seniors and especially in reading. "The 1994 reading scores are woeful," said Chester E. Finn Jr., a member of the National Assessment's Governing Board and former Assistant Secretary of Education. "Only one high school senior in three was a 'proficient' reader in 1994. . . . Almost as many—30 percent—were 'below basic,' significant erosion from 1992's 25 percent. 'Below basic' means essentially non-functional as readers, even though the young people taking the test were within a few months of graduating. And that means [1994's] graduation ceremonies dumped about 750,000 more semi-literate 18-year-olds into the work force with high school diplomas clutched in their fists."[36]

Of black high school seniors, 54 percent were "below basic"; of Hispanic, 48 percent.[37] Yet as Finn points out, "Weak performance is by no means confined to poor and minority youngsters or inner-city schools. In upscale Montgomery County, Maryland, where nearly everybody graduates from high school and 86 percent go on to higher education, the local community college found that 71% of students entering from county schools were deficient in math and half failed to meet the English standards."[38]

On an encouraging note, from 1910 to 1993 the percentage of Americans with four or more years of college had risen from 2.7 to 21.9 percent; and those with four years of high school, from 13.5 to 81.5 percent.[39] Yet, over almost the same period, illiteracy paradoxically doubled.[40] In 1900, 10.7 percent of adult Americans were unable to read or write a simple sentence in any language.[41] By 1993, that 10.7 had become 21 percent.[42] In fact, a recent survey of two hundred major corporations showed they had to teach 22 percent of their employees how to read, 41 percent how to write, and 31 percent how to do math.[43] When tested, only forty-seven Americans out of a hundred could put together or compare facts from different pieces of information.[44] In addition, according to a 1998 *Wall Street Journal* front-page report, "About 30 percent of first-time college students take remedial courses because they can't read, write or do math adequately."[45] In the California State University system, the figure is between 70 and 90 percent.[46] In New York State community colleges, 87 percent of entering students flunk the very placement test that would qualify them to do remedial work.[47]

Literacy, to be sure, is a critical skill, one that we need for work. But literacy is more than that too, for without it we remain cut off from a wider world of knowledge and ideas. Words are the precious lifeline that connects us with current events and with the experience and wisdom of earlier times. And the less literate we are, the looser the grip we have on that line.

Yet even more pernicious than illiteracy is *a*literacy.[48] The illiterate person is someone who cannot read; the aliterate, someone who knows how to read but doesn't want to. For the illiterate, a library is an important building with a locked door; for the aliterate, both the door and the building have lost all significance. Sadly, tests have demonstrated the existence of both conditions among prospective graduates of America's high schools and colleges.

Ever since 1926, the Scholastic Aptitude Test, or SAT, has been used as a standard admissions test by America's colleges and universities. In 1941, the average score on the verbal part and the math part was 500 each, halfway between 200 and 800, the extremes of the grading scale.[49]

Since 1941, however, average scores on both parts have been dropping.[50] In 1994, the verbal average had fallen seventy-six points; the math average, twenty-two.[51]

Some argued that the decline reflected demographics.[52] Back in 1941, there were only ten thousand test-takers, mostly wealthy and well-educated white young men from the Northeast. By 1994, almost two million students, male and female, were taking the test, a far larger and also a far more racially and economically diverse group.

Despite the differences, however, even the best students were becoming less knowledgeable. Over one twelve–year period, for example, the number of students who scored above 650 fell by 73 percent.[53]

Nevertheless, in response to changes in the student population, the College Board decided to make the test easier: beginning with 1995, fewer questions had to be answered, more time (thirty minutes more) would be given to answer them, calculators could be used for math problems, and the dreaded antonym section would disappear.[54]

In addition, it was decided to "recenter," or recalibrate, the scoring system, boosting the typical test-taker's score on the verbal part by eighty points, and the math part by twenty.[55] In effect, students would get a one hundred-point bonus for just showing up at the test site.[56] Besides this, the College Board also changed the definition of "perfect." Students could now get a "perfect" score even if they missed as many as four questions.[57]

Because of these changes, it will forever be impossible to compare the competence of students who took the test before and after 1995. Referring to the new scores on the verbal test, critic Diane Ravitch stated: "The College Board has turned . . . deplorable performance . . . into a new norm. The old average was a standard that American education aspired to meet; the new average validates mediocrity."[58] Bruno V. Manno, senior fellow at the Hudson Institute, succinctly summed it up this way: "The S.A.T. results are one more example of how we're defining excellence down."[59]

If knowing who you are in a cultural sense also means being familiar with traditional literature, many Americans—including those called educated—have far to go. In a survey by the National Endowment for the Humanities,[60] only 42 percent of college seniors knew Plato wrote *The Republic*, only 56 percent knew Melville wrote *Moby Dick*, and only 58 percent knew the Koran is the sacred text of Islam. Picking the right answer on an NEH multiple-choice test is one thing; knowing the real substance of these works is something else. How many graduating seniors had really read and thought about these works is something we may never know, but the percentages would probably be far lower.

MAKING THE CONNECTIONS

Higher education must surely do more than teach some students the right answers to a short-answer test on civilization. Education's larger purpose must be to teach them why those answers are worth knowing. But even that will not be enough. Colleges and universities must also teach their students the cultural whole to which the parts belong. Knowing isolated facts alone is insufficient, for only when students understand their interconnections can they appreciate their full significance.

This same truth underlies the nature of personal identity. We most easily remember things through a process of association, and it is this web of associations that constitutes the fabric of who we are.

Some years ago our son—by way of giving his parents an anniversary present—pored through shoe boxes and envelopes of old family photos to create a collage that now hangs on our living room wall. Looking at it now, my wife and I can see ourselves and our children in birthdays and baby pictures, in family get-togethers and graduations, over the course of some twenty years.

The collage is composed not by chronology but only by color and form. The meaning of the scattered pieces lies in the fact that each is a part of a greater whole—the life of a family that still lives. As important as the separate moments are in themselves, more important still is the invisible bond that connects them. For without this spiritual or emotional "glue," each is but a fragment stripped of its most vital dimension of meaning.

Memory, and with it our personal identity, is more than the sum of random mnemonic parts, but a whole greater and deeper than that sum. Questions like ones we have already asked—"Do you know where you are?" "Do you know what day it is?" "Do you remember your name?"—even if they elicit answers, can only superficially serve to test the memory of a victim of amnesia, not restore to her or him a sense of psychological wholeness and well-being.

Our real personal lives, the true substance of our identity, is to be found in something far more precious and also far more elusive and subtle than such data. If it is to be found anywhere, it is to be discovered in the resonance between separate facts and in the invisible bonds that hold them together, bonds that cannot be so readily articulated but are no less actual because of that.

Thus, if higher education only teaches the "who," "what," "where," and "when" of our common heritage without also pointing out the "why," it will have failed to instruct students in the meaning of their humanity. And yet it is in precisely this way that higher education has been failing young Americans for decades.

In 1989, only 35 percent of teachers in America's colleges and universities believed "it is essential or very important to teach students the classic works of Western civilization."[61] Six years later, in 1995, the percentage had dropped to 28 percent.[62] In another more recent study, out of twenty-five prominent liberal arts colleges in the nation, only five were requiring their English majors to read Shakespeare.[63]

In 1996, the National Association of Scholars (NAS) issued a report summarizing its review of undergraduate education in America over the course of the last century.[64] Drawing its data from the catalogues of the fifty most selective colleges and universities in the country, the NAS study focused on those basic courses that were required for a student to be awarded a bachelor of arts (B.A.) degree in 1914, 1939, 1964, and 1993. The first three years were chosen because they were landmark dates in the social and political history of the United States; 1993, because it was the most recent year for which complete catalogues were available. The courses required in each of those years would constitute a "snapshot" of what it then meant to be an educated person in the eyes of America's most distinguished institutions of higher learning.

The NAS found that American higher education had virtually abandoned core courses.[65] The percentage of institutions requiring history for graduation had shrunk from 41 percent in 1914 to 12 percent in 1993; those requiring literature had declined from 57 percent in 1914 to 14 percent in 1993. Thus, in 1993, a student could graduate from 88 percent of America's best colleges and universities without ever having had to study history and from 86 percent without ever having studied literature. And these were America's *best* colleges and universities. As the report concluded: "If [academic institutions] can no longer define educational essentials—and, in particular, no longer guarantee that students acquire a basic knowledge of their civilization and heritage—we are in danger of losing the common frame of cultural reference that for many generations has sustained our liberal, democratic society. . . . Answers must be found if our country is not to end up paying an extraordinarily high price."[66]

THE COST OF FORGETTING

There is obviously a difference between forgetting what you once knew and not knowing what you were never taught. Perhaps, therefore, the notion of cultural "amnesia" is a misnomer. If people never learned these things in the first place, how can we claim they "forgot" them?

Naturally, we can't. But my larger purpose is to examine not individuals but rather cultures—specifically, *our* culture. The life of an individual is measured in years and decades; the life of a culture, in centuries and even millennia. A culture maintains its identity by passing on the sum of its values and experiences from one generation to the next. Its memory must be organic and transtemporal, else the culture dies or survives only as a hollow shell. A culture is like a tree—its leaves and branches reaching skyward toward the future, its trunk fixed solidly in the present, its roots drawing nourishment from a subterranean past. Continuity is therefore at the very heart of what civilization is. As Civil War historian Bruce Catton has written of America: "The great American story is above all other things a *continued* story. It did not start with us and will not end with us."[67]

From its very origins, the emergence of civilization was associated with the invention of writing and the development of a vocabulary whose precision was matched to society's own complexity. The birth of civilization was also associated with the creation of a literature in which those words, and the experiences they contained, were enshrined. In inverse fashion, as a civilization declines, its people lose touch with those instruments and their meaning. Thus illiteracy—the disenfranchisement from the written word and its wisdom—becomes tantamount to expatriation.

In 1816, Thomas Jefferson had warned: "If a nation expects to be ignorant and free, in a state of civilization, it expects what never was and never will be."[68] Today, when so many Americans can be numbered as victims of cultural amnesia, his words have particular relevancy for the future of our nation.

A decade of statistics about the ignorance of our students and the shortcomings of our schools is not, after all, just an indictment of an educational process gone wrong. Since every high school and college graduate goes on to become a potential husband, wife, parent, worker, and voter, the statistics also constitute an indictment of the kind of society we have been creating. Ignorance of geography and history, illiteracy and aliteracy, thus do not just represent wrong answers on some Gallup poll or national survey; instead, they draw a composite sketch of contemporary American identity and the future of the American mind. And if the ignorant students of today go on to become the ignorant teachers of tomorrow, our national amnesia can only grow worse.

Can Americans, for example, preserve their free institutions and build a better society in peacetime if they have forgotten democracy's value and price? How can they recognize liberty as something rare and precious and easily lost if they have forgotten both the words and meaning of the documents upon which American democracy was founded, and if they have only the most minimal understanding of the sacrifices that were needed to bring those ideas closer to reality?

Furthermore, how can Americans deal with the issue of war if they have but the blurriest notion of the wars already fought? How can the very subject of war be understood if the basic facts of past wars have been forgotten—the names, the dates, the battles, the causes, and the consequences? Indeed, how can Americans wisely choose between fighting and not fighting if, on the one hand, they have forgotten war's human cost and if, on the other, they have never learned the historical necessity of giving one's life in order to preserve a way of life for others?

Ignorance, after all, is not merely a state of innocence. If deliberate, it becomes an act of complicity, enabling others to control our lives. If unintentional, it nevertheless makes us vulnerable to others' will.

In George Orwell's *1984*, the "mutability of the past" was the "central tenet" of society.[69] In Orwell's imaginary dictatorship, the past was continually altered and realtered as an instrument of political policy.

> The alteration of the past is necessary for two reasons. . . . The Party member, like the proletarian, tolerates present-day conditions partly because he has no standards of comparison. He must be cut off from the past . . . because it is necessary for him to believe that he is better off than his ancestors and that the average level of material comfort is continually rising. But by far the more important reason for the readjustment of the past is the need to safeguard the infallibility of the Party.[70]

In the land of the Lotus-eaters, however, such a policy is not even required. Moneyed interests and those with political power can today take comfort in the fact that America's cultural memory tape is self-erasing. In Lotus-land, the longest of memories is but short-term.

But memory is not just a defense against totalitarianism, imaginary or real. It can also be the active means to our further liberation, a reservoir of energy from which we can draw a renewed sense of direction and purpose. As one contemporary social critic has put it: "The past, even if it is not superior in total to the present, can nonetheless serve as a reminder of values we are neglecting and parts of ourselves with which we have lost contact."[71]

Surely we must not romanticize the past; but, even more importantly, we must not become oblivious to it. Romanticizing the past may unnecessarily denigrate the present and our own achievements in it; but forgetting the past altogether means we will have lost the one enduring standard by which we can measure where we are and how far we have yet to go.

Psychologist Havelock Ellis once said that civilization is the art of holding on and letting go.[72] But for every letting go there is a price. How will we remain civilized if memory is the price? And what will our civilization be like if we no longer remember?

CHAPTER 2

MEMORY AND PERSONAL
IDENTITY

At 12:20 on the morning of August 31, 1997, a sleek Mercedes hurtled down a tunnel beneath the streets of Paris, struck a support column, and careened into a wall. Three people were killed: Diana, Princess of Wales; her companion, Emad "Dodi" al-Fayed; and the driver, Henri Paul. Only one passenger survived—Trevor Rees-Jones, a bodyguard employed by the Fayed family.

At the same moment thousands of miles away in Chicago, my wife and I slept in a small motel. Waking in the early morning, we turned on the television set and saw the first reports of the Paris accident and, later, the graphic account of Diana's death.

Like those (and I am one of them) who vividly recall where they were when they first learned of President Kennedy's assassination, I remember where I was when I first learned of Diana's death. I remember the motel and the room, even the location of the television set we watched from our bed.

The sole survivor of the collision, Trevor Rees-Jones, still bears scars from the crash on the left side of his face. But he also bears an invisible scar within the dark recesses of his brain. Interrogated about the crash ("Why were you going so fast? Was your driver drunk? Did another vehicle cut you off?"), he can remember little of the moments before the accident. Though he was an eyewitness, the eyes of his memory are blind and may never recapture that fatal vision.

Why do I recall the accident so vividly and in such detail, even though I was thousands of miles away? And why can't he do so, who was in the very car? These are among memory's mysteries we will explore in this chapter.

THE CAUSES OF AMNESIA[1]

An Assault upon the Brain

The absence of memory, or amnesia, can be caused by an assault upon the brain. Such an assault can take many forms.

Physical Injury. In the case of Rees-Jones, the cause was physical trauma, an injury sustained by his brain from a blow to the head that occurred at impact. For younger victims of amnesia, this is the most common cause: a closed-head injury sustained in an automobile accident. Such injuries can erase the memory of the events immediately before an accident or, sometimes, the memory of events that occurred days, months, or even years before. As the brain heals, many memories return, but others do not. According to one theory, the moments before the crash are the ones most readily forgotten—either because memories of them have not yet taken structural form in the mind, or because the neural paths for their retrieval have not yet been laid down. Hence, of all memories, the most recent are the most fragile.

Electrical Shock. But amnesia can be caused by other types of assault. An intense electrical current, for example, can figuratively burn out the wiring of the brain. Such a shock can come from inside or outside. A short circuit can occur spontaneously within the brain during a convulsion; or a jolt of current can be deliberately applied by a therapist to shock the personality into equilibrium. Either way, the electric bill is paid for in the currency of memory.

Disease and Stroke. Remembrance can also be ravaged by disease—by herpes simplex encephalitis, that inflames and swells the brain's delicate tissue; or by the most devastating of mnemonic maladies, Alzheimer's disease, that turns the brain to cellular mush. Stroke and anemia can likewise wreak havoc by robbing brain cells of life-giving oxygen.

Self-induced Oblivion

Ironically, the very memories that encapsulate personal experience can be expunged by personal behavior. The alcoholic, seeking temporary oblivion in a bottle, may find it in more permanent form in Korsakoff's syndrome, a set of symptoms first described by a nineteenth-century Russian psychologist. Confusion and disorientation are its first signs, the result of poor nutrition and thiamine deficiency that can accompany chronic alcoholism. If not treated soon enough, the outcome is permanent memory loss.

Psychogenic Amnesia

Memory loss can also be triggered by emotional crisis and the need to forget. In running away from an experience too painful to remember, we may bolt through an emergency exit in our consciousness, locking the steel door—and the memory—behind us. If the experience is terribly traumatic, we may even try to escape from our own identity. Called a fugue state, such a condition is very rare, accounting for only about 1 percent of all amnesias, though amid the horrors of war and combat the frequency can be much higher.[2] In a fugue state, all autobiographical memory vanishes, but other kinds of memory persist: you know Manhattan is in New York, but you don't know who you are or why you are there. In time—days, weeks, or months—personal memory and, with it, a sense of individual identity almost always return. As time heals, the psyche gains the strength and courage to look into the mirror of the past.

It's Natural to Forget

Leaving Pain Behind. Novelist Sholem Asch once wrote: "Not the power to remember, but its very opposite, the power to forget, is a necessary condition for our existence."[3] We need not enter a fugue state to acknowledge there are some things best forgotten. In everyone's life there is pain, but to remember all the painful experiences in our lives would make existence itself intolerable. Feeding on guilt or dwelling on hurt can only keep us from discovering the joys that may still await us. Indeed, one may argue, as has Asch, that forgetting is nature's way of helping us to go on living.

Coping with Stimuli. Nor is it only the painful incidents of life we must forget. Each day, each second, our senses are bombarded with stimuli. To respond to some, we must ignore others, else our existence would become a blur in which nothing—no face, no voice, no sensory experience—would be distinct. To remember everything would mean to drown in the waters of memory, waters which—if we would drink them one sip at a time—could nourish our souls. Like the principal character in Jorge Luis Borges's short story, "Funes, the Memorious,"[4] we would lose our sense of self, engulfed in a sea roiling with mnemonic flotsam and jetsam.

Growing Up. Already, a whole part of our life lies unremembered—the time in our childhood before we turned three or four. The missing memories from this period are due to infantile amnesia, a natural effect of the brain's underdevelopment. Only when we are older, when the circuitry of the brain has been firmly established, will we begin to build true memories. The recollections we may have of earlier events (a birthday party, a trip to the zoo) are more likely based on what we were later told by loving relatives or later saw in family photo albums or home movies. Eventually, the events became so familiar, it seemed that we "remembered" them too.

Growing Old. At the other end of the biological spectrum, aging often weakens the function of memory, but for healthy and active people, far less than we might imagine.[5] As the human brain ages and its cells die, some mental powers do decline, but others remain strong.

In late life it is the most distant memories that can seem the clearest. In reviewing their lives and searching for patterns of meaning, the elderly can derive that rare but underrated commodity called wisdom.[6] Yet if there is too little to look forward to, the aging mind can atrophy and the power of memory degrade, for when the parameters of experience contract, the sense of identity shrinks as well, as though conforming to the strictures of a smaller life. In the cruelest of dementias, elderly victims rage against the dying of the light until they are imprisoned within a cranial darkness that extinguishes the last candle of the self.

VARIETIES OF AMNESIA

When we think of an amnesia victim, we think of a person who doesn't remember who he or she *is*. But, in actuality, who you are is really who you *were*.

If you were to ask me who I am, I might facetiously reply that I am an adult male Earthling, 5 feet 10½ inches in height (I omit the weight), with brown eyes and (alas) now graying hair. But that is not so much *who* I am as *what* I am.

Interrogated further, I might tell you my name, or where I live, or what work I do. But all those facets of my identity emanate from the past: the name my parents gave me, the house my wife and I bought, the job I was hired to do. In the truest sense, who I am now is an extension of an earlier self.

So when amnesia victims forget who they *are*, they are really forgetting who they *were*. Their malady is that they have lost the vital link between present and past.

Retrograde Amnesia

The kind of amnesia most familiar to us is known as "retrograde amnesia," a forgetting of those experiences that preceded the amnesia's onset. The patient awakens in the hospital and can't remember how she got there. She may have also forgotten facts of a less personal nature: the name of the president of the United States, or the current month and year. Like a recording tape that has been erased, the memory tape of her mind is blank. To be sure, new memories can be recorded on it, but the old ones are wiped clean, gone forever unless time, patience, and skill can somehow restore them.

The good news is that, in most cases of retrograde amnesia, the memories *do* return; their permanent loss is very rare.

Yet for some victims of retrograde amnesia, like mythical Tantalus tortured in Hades, memories are forever beyond reach. Psychologist Daniel L. Schacter describes one such victim:

> A head injury patient I once interviewed who had lost many treasured memories felt that he had also lost his sense of self. He became so obsessed with the missing pages of his past that he could think or talk of little else.
> "I can't review my life," he kept telling me.[7]

Another patient, a survivor of a motorcycle accident, retained a general knowledge of life but forgot the part he himself had played in it. Cell biologist Rebecca Rupp reports:

> His mind is a dictionary rather than a scrapbook; an instruction manual rather than an autobiography. He knows what a Christmas tree is, but remembers no Christmases; he knows that leaves turn color in the fall, but remembers no walks through the woods; he can identify a daffodil, but remembers no springs. His personal past is gone.[8]

Anterograde Amnesia

In retrograde amnesia, the recording tape of the past has been erased. In anterograde amnesia, it is the tape recorder itself that is broken. The sights and sounds of the past remain on the cassette, but nothing new can be added.

Thus, victims of anterograde amnesia have a clear recollection of their lives before the "amnesic event"; they just can't recall anything that happened since. As psychologist Alan Baddeley notes: "You could spend all morning with such a patient who would then fail to recognize you in the afternoon."[9]

"The Man with the Teflon Brain." The most famous example of such a patient is a man known for the sake of confidentiality as Henry M.[10]—"the patient most studied in the history of medical literature,"[11] "arguably the single most important patient ever studied in neuropsychology,"[12] or, more simply, "the man with the Teflon brain."

In 1953, in an ill-conceived act of experimental brain surgery intended to relieve epileptic seizures, a surgeon using suction removed a fist-sized portion from the center of Henry's brain. "In one sharp intake of air he lost the world,"[13] for what was stolen from him was his ability to remember.

> Because of his condition . . . it was possible for him to read a newspaper or magazine, put it down, and then twenty minutes later pick it up fresh again. He might well read it over and over, each time for the first time. The date on the cover would be no help, as he hadn't the faintest notion of what the day, the month, or year was. . . . Each morning . . . he woke and did not know where he was. . . . He had been in this state since 1953, and did not know that fact either. There was almost nothing before or behind him; he was perpetually held in one moment, a moment resembling that instant when we wake from a particularly heavy sleep and cannot recall just where we are, or just what business we are about.[14]

As Henry himself reflected one day, revealing the gentleness and frailty of his soul:

> Right now, I'm wondering, have I done or said anything amiss? You see, at this moment everything looks clear to me, but what happened just before? That's what worries me. It's like waking from a dream; I just don't remember. . . . Every day is alone, in itself. Whatever enjoyment I've had, and whatever sorrow I've had.[15]

More poignant still is the case of M.P., another victim of anterograde amnesia.[16] Each time he hears of his father's death, he cries as though hearing it for the first time.

Global Amnesia

In a few patients, retrograde and anterograde amnesia are combined, but the rare condition is usually transient, lasting only for hours. For a very few patients, however, the condition persists. If, in addition, the retrograde amnesia is only partial, the patient becomes trapped in a slice of the past, the only portion of his experience he will ever remember.

Such was the case for Stephen R., who suffered from Korsakoff's syndrome as well as other neurological conditions. Psychologist Oliver Sacks recounts the tale:

In hospital he could recognise nobody and nothing, and was in an almost ceaseless frenzy of disorientation. But when his wife took him home, to his house which was in effect a "time-capsule" of his pre-amnesia days, he felt instantly at home. He recognized everything, tapped the barometer, checked the thermostat, took his favourite armchair, as he used to do. He spoke of neighbors, shops, the local pub, a nearby cinema, as they had been in the mid-Seventies. He was distressed and puzzled if the smallest changes were made in the house. ("You changed the curtains today!" he once expostulated to his wife. "How come? So suddenly? They were green this morning." But they had not been green since 1978.) He recognised most of the neighbouring houses and shops—they had changed little between 1978 and 1983—but was bewildered by the "replacement" of the cinema ("How could they tear it down and put up a supermarket *overnight?*") He recognized friends and neighbours—but found them oddly older than he expected ("Old so-and-so! He's really showing his age. Never noticed it before. How come everyone's showing their age today?"). But the real poignancy, the horror, would occur when his wife brought him back—brought him, in a fantastic and unaccountable manner (so he felt), to a strange home he had never seen, full of strangers, and then left him. "What are you doing?" he would scream, terrified and confused. "What in the hell *is* this place? What the hell's going on?" These scenes were almost unbearable to watch, and must have seemed like madness, or nightmare, to the patient. Mercifully perhaps he would forget them within a couple of minutes.[17]

VARIETIES OF MEMORY

Just as there are different kinds of amnesia, so are there different types of memory.

Psychologists generally distinguish three main types based upon their content: episodic, semantic, and procedural. Episodic memories are the memories of earlier experiences and events in our lives. Semantic memories represent the general knowledge and information we have acquired. Procedural memories embody the practical skills we have learned—for example, how to drive a car. Psychologists sometimes use the term "declarative," or "explicit," to describe episodic and semantic memories since we are consciously aware of their presence when we draw upon them; whereas they apply the term "nondeclarative," or "implicit," to describe procedural memories (and others) of which we are less consciously aware.

In addition to content, memories are also categorized by their duration. As the term suggests, short-term memories are temporary, while long-term memories are more lasting. A subcategory of short-term memory is working memory, the "Post-it" of the mind, that holds information (such as a telephone number we've just looked up) only so long as we need it, and then promptly discards it (after we've dialed). In reality, short-term and long-term memories are best understood as a continuum, since many so-called short-term memories can last for many months, and some so-called long-term memories stay dormant until, with the right prompting, we summon them up.

Different types of memory can, in fact, be damaged by different types of amnesia. For example, psychogenic amnesia, brought on by an emotional crisis, may block episodic memory but leave semantic and procedural memory intact. (We might, for example, forget our name, but we would still remember how to drive a car and get to the airport.) Alzheimer's disease, on the other hand, erodes both episodic and semantic memory.

INVESTIGATIVE TECHNIQUES

The terminology above is a convenient means of rationally classifying what still remains an essentially mysterious process. As Alan Baddeley puts it: "Psychologists investigating memory are largely in the position of someone trying to understand the functioning of a machine without being able to look inside it."[18]

Test Results

Consequently, psychologists over the years have used various testing methods on subjects to discover the strengths and weaknesses of human memory. Some of the results have a practical application, revealing strategies we can apply to improve our memory.[19] Other results are fascinating for what they disclose about the workings of the mind: first, that memory is *conceptual*—the things we remember best are the ones whose threads we can weave into knowledge we already possess; second, that memory is *contextual*—we recall things best if we are in the same environment in which we first learned them; and third, that memory is *emotional*—the things we remember most are the things that have had an emotional impact upon us. Thus, if an event is shocking enough (like Princess Diana's or President Kennedy's sudden death), the incident and the circumstances surrounding it can sear themselves into our consciousness in a phenomenon known as "flashbulb memory."

Studies have also shown that subjects can be convincingly implanted with memories of experiences they never actually had[20]; furthermore, that our memories undergo continual revision, colored by later knowledge and by the image of our past selves we would prefer to see. Rather than being objective and concrete, memory is subjective and malleable.

A Window on the Brain

Despite earlier limitations, newer investigative techniques now allow neuroscientists to gaze through a window on the brain.[21] As a consequence of their stunning discoveries (discoveries that, incidentally, still continue), "in the last two decades greater progress has been made in understanding memory than in the previous 3,000."[22]

Foremost among these techniques are sophisticated electronic brain scans using computerized tomography (CAT), functional magnetic resonance imaging (MRI), and positron emission tomography (PET). CAT scans portray with photographic detail the brain structures of living subjects; MRIs measure changes in the flow rate of oxygen-bearing blood; and PETs chart the radioactive path of energy-giving glucose. Together, MRIs and PETs make various structures in the brain "light up" when they work, revealing the sites that play key roles in learning and memory.

Yet as dazzling as such scans may be, they disclose only part of the story. If, for example, we were asked what part of a television set is responsible for the picture, we might name the picture tube. In actuality, however, a whole array of transistorized components and circuits collaborate with the tube to produce the image on the screen. Likewise, the process of storing and retrieving memories may well depend upon many parts of the brain working in concert, parts that may be less conspicuous than others but are nonetheless just as important.

THE STRUCTURE OF MEMORY

A Universe Within

In a single brain weighing three or four pounds there are as many as a hundred billion nerve cells, or neurons—as many as the stars in the Milky Way. Yet, unlike the stars, all of these neurons are interconnected in a vast network. Were we to try to count all of the neural junctures in our brain at the rate of one per second, it would take us more than half a million lifetimes.

The myriad cells of the brain communicate by an electrochemical process. Each neuron possesses a stemlike sending unit called an axon, and a branchlike set of antennas called dendrites. A chemically-induced electrical charge travels down the length of the axon, releasing molecules that are then picked up by the dendrites of an adjoining neuron. Thus, in a split second, messages travel from one cell to another across a narrow gap called the synapse. The more the synapse is activated, the stronger the connection grows, and the more enduring the intercellular bond becomes.

It is hard to say where a particular memory might be stored in the brain. In fact, recent research suggests a memory may be a composite fused together from different signals simultaneously transmitted from a number of specialized sites. What *is* known is that the hippocampus, a sea-horse-shaped organ located deep in the brain, plays a critical role in memory formation. It was this very organ that was tragically removed from the head of Henry M.

Enemies of the Brain

The delicate structure of the brain can be deformed by stress and disease. Chronic stress can produce changes in the brain's chemistry, pumping out hormones that erode the connections between neurons and shrink the hippocampus by starving it of oxygen.[23] Alzheimer's disease, for its part, invades the brain with abnormal proteins.[24] Like clumps of seaweed in a neural Sargasso sea, they choke off cells and clog their synapses, killing off both the hippocampus and the cortex, seat of reasoning and judgment. Though its cause remains unknown, Alzheimer's sudden appearance in our century may mark it, along with stress, as a byproduct of a technological society that daily tests our biologically adaptive limits.

The Enigma of Memory

Yet even the healthy brain remains an enigma. That a fusillade of insensate molecules could simulate the melody of a remembered song or the moment of a first kiss seems for now, at least to this writer, most improbable. As with many reductionist scenarios, the psychic whole may turn out to be more than the sum of its physical parts.

What we do know is that the linkages of memory provide what Nobel laureate John Eccles called "the continuity of self,"[25] the subtle joining not of impersonal axons and dendrites but of personal present and past. Between the delicate tendrils of the dendrite and the axon arms reaching out to them lies the elusive hologram of the self projected onto the membrane of the mind.

> Without [memory], we are hollow persons, not only empty of a past, but lacking a foundation upon which to build the future. We are what we remember.[26]

CHAPTER 3

MEMORY AND
CIVILIZATION

Like a person, a culture also has a memory, but cultural memory is different from personal memory in two ways. Instead of representing the memory of a single individual, it constitutes the collective memory of many; and instead of being contained within the compass of a single lifetime, it can encompass generations. Thus the memory of a culture is both broader and deeper than that of an individual.

But there is another difference as well: cultural memory requires transmission—from person to person, and century to century. Unlike the vivid personal memories brought to us by our own experience, cultural memory comes to us secondhand. Therein also lies cultural memory's peculiar vulnerability, for if the memories of the past are not passed on, for all intents and purposes they cease to exist.

In previous chapters we have seen that an individual's identity depends upon an organic and conscious connection between the present and the past, that without such a vital connection personal life itself is diminished. If this is true of an individual, it may also be true of a civilization whose life may likewise depend upon such continuity. Indeed, it may be argued that, if nothing else, the history of civilization is the history of remembrance.

To fully appreciate the interconnection between memory and civilization, we will need to travel back into time—in fact to a time before civilization itself began.

FROM THE STONE AGE TO THE SISTINE CHAPEL

Echoes from the Cave

Regardless of human artifice or intention, the memory of a life can sometimes persist like a fingerprint unwittingly left behind.

Prehistoric times are those from which no written record comes because writing itself had not yet been invented. Nevertheless, a record of these times does exist, not in words but in scattered spear points and abandoned campfires. These remains testify to the harsh realities of primitive life and to the fact that a knowledge of tradition made survival possible, for surviving meant drawing upon ancestral wisdom: the skill of capturing fire and, later, creating it with friction; the lore of plants, telling which could cure or kill and which could nourish; the craft of fashioning rough stones into keen-edged blades; and the art of the hunter, tracking and stalking his prey.

The Stone Age hunt was memorialized in Europe on the walls of caves. There painters portrayed the awesome images of charging bison and herds of fleet horse and deer.[1]

Some murals have been found at the entrances of caves or under overhangs, but most are hidden in the depths of caves. Some works were executed in spacious corridors or easily accessible rooms, near or far from daylight. Others—the majority—were produced under extraordinary conditions, hundreds of yards from the entrance, beyond whirlpools or difficult passageways, in recesses where the artist had to work from a prone position, in spiralling tunnels where he had to crawl like a cat and inch his way upward like a chimney-sweep. Obviously, the artist did not make his way into such places and paint the walls just for pastime: simply by their location, these works suggest the existence of sanctuaries.[2]

To such sanctuaries the young hunters of the tribe were led to be initiated into manhood. Huddled together, they would have heard from their elders tales of the great hunts and hunters of the past, tales designed to inspire them to become great hunters too. There in the darkness, the flickering light of the torches made the painted images of the mighty beasts come alive before them. In the blaze of fire, past became present.

For tens of thousands of years, primitive cultures passed on their traditions this way—by word of mouth and artistic representation. But the chain of tradition depended upon living links, or "rememberers." Without someone to tell the tale or explain the picture, the story would be forgotten. And if the story was forgotten, the culture would lose its way.

Though it is easy to think of simple societies as living a spontaneous existence in the here and now, such a view is all too superficial because it fails to take account of the way the past undergirded the present.[3]

The Invention of Writing

Twenty-five thousand years after the first European cave paintings were made, humanity entered a new era. In the fertile river valleys of the Near East—the Nile in Egypt, the Tigris and Euphrates in Iraq—a form of society arose called civilization.

Civilization's most distinguishing traits were its social complexity and wealth, a wealth based on agricultural abundance.[4] Power was vested in kings who ruled populous nation-states maintained by armies and enlarged by conquest. At the same time, authoritarian priesthoods administered rich temples and estates in the name of the gods.

One of the consequences of civilization was the invention of writing. Writing enabled kings to chronicle their victories and priests to inscribe their prayers. But, above all, writing enabled both groups to catalogue their growing wealth. Thus materialism, more than god or country, was responsible for writing's beginnings.[5]

Some people, however, were suspicious of the new technology. According to a tale preserved by Plato, an Egyptian pharaoh was among the doubters. In a dialogue called *Phaedrus*, the Greek philosopher relates the following account:

> At the Egyptian city of Naucratis, there was a famous old god, whose name was Thoth; the bird which is called the ibis is sacred to him, and he was the inventor of many arts, such as arithmetic and calculation and geometry and astronomy and draughts and dice, but his greatest discovery was the use of writing. Now in those days Thamus was the king of the whole of Upper Egypt, which is the district surrounding that great city which is called by the Hellenes Egyptian Thebes. . . .
>
> Thoth came to Thamus and showed his inventions, desiring that the other Egyptians might be allowed to have the benefit of them; he went through them, and Thamus inquired about their several uses, and praised some of them and censured others, as he approved or disapproved of them. There would be no use in repeating all that Thamus said to Thoth in praise or blame of the various arts. But when they

came to writing, Thoth said: "This will make the Egyptians wiser and give them better memories: for I have found the elixir of memory and wisdom." Thamus replied: "O most ingenious Thoth, he who has the gift of invention is not always the best judge of the utility or inutility of his own inventions to the users of them. And in this instance a paternal love of your own child has led you to say what is not the fact; for this invention of yours will create forgetfulness in the learners' souls, because they will not use their memories; they will trust to the external written characters and not remember of themselves. You have found an elixir not of remembering but of being reminded, and you give your disciples only the pretense of wisdom; they will be hearers of many things but will have understood nothing; they will appear to be omniscient but will in fact know little; and they will be difficult to deal with, since they will have the reputation for knowledge without the reality."[6]

If Plato's account is based on genuine Egyptian tradition, such qualms failed to prevent the technology of writing from gaining acceptance, for writing became one of the hallmarks of civilization. Emerging from a cluster of simple pictograms (drawings of people and things), the hieroglyphic script of Egypt and the cuneiform script of Mesopotamia evolved into elaborate systems comprised of hundreds upon hundreds of distinct characters representing diverse sounds and ideas. So complex were these systems that many years of intense training were required simply to read or write. An entire class of workers, known as scribes, thus arose to serve the needs of palace and temple.

Literacy was by no means universal. Indeed, the very complexity of the systems shut out the masses from knowledge and protected the elite, who became the official guardians of cultural memory. Still, ancestral custom and ritual as well as stories passed on by word of mouth kept popular tradition alive. Many of these stories, in fact, were eventually written down by scribes, who thereby created the world's first literature.

Though temple and palace archives had long existed in the Near East, a seventh century B.C. king of Assyria named Ashurbanipal may have been the first to create a personal library. To carry out his plan, Ashurbanipal ordered his scribes to travel far and wide across the land in search of works to copy. On a cuneiform inscription which still survives, the king's voice proclaims:

I, Ashurbanipal, within the palace understood the wisdom of Nebo (god of learning); all the art of writing of every craftsman, of every kind, I made myself the master of them all. . . . Among the kings who have gone before, no one ever acquired that craft. . . . I read the cunning tablets of Sumer, and the dark Akkadian language which is difficult rightly to use; I took my pleasure in reading stones inscribed before the flood."[7]

But for all of Ashurbanipal's zeal, his was a private not a public library. Today, the twenty-six thousand inscribed tablets from his royal collection constitute one of the treasures of London's British Museum, where they were deposited after being uncovered by archaeologists in 1852. Among the works are legends of the gods, tales of heroic adventure, historical annals, scientific texts, and a category known as wisdom literature, containing traditional observations on the human condition.

Technical complexity notwithstanding, writing's invention represented a tremendous leap forward in the preservation and transmission of human experience. Previously, knowledge had to be conveyed from one living person to another through the oral interpretation of pictures or through the spoken word. Now human experience could, in effect, speak for itself without the need for an interpreter. Moreover, the fact that experience could be transcribed onto materials more durable than flesh gave it a longevity it never before possessed. Long after a scribe's death, the words he had brushed onto papyrus or impressed into clay could live on, available to generations hundreds or even thousands of years later. In a library a single individual could draw upon the collective wisdom of the ages.

Literacy, however, was still severely limited both by writing's complex nature and society's own rigid class structure. It would take another extraordinary invention to change all that.

The Coming of the Alphabet

That invention, like so many others down through history, was based on an amazingly simple principle. Instead of depending upon hundreds of specialized characters, the total number was reduced to the couple of dozen that represented the sounds all words had in common. Each character would then stand for a single consonant or vowel. By rearranging these basic signs in different combinations, a writer could reproduce a language's every word.

When and where the first alphabet was devised is hard to say.[8] Inscriptional evidence points to sometime in the second millennium B.C., with experimentation taking place in Syria, Lebanon, and Israel, lands where innovation was not stifled by the dominance of older writing systems.

By the ninth century B.C., enterprising Phoenician traders were sailing from ports like Byblos and Sidon in boats equipped not only with merchandise but a streamlined twenty-two–letter alphabet that let every ship's captain keep track of his cargo and transactions. When the Phoenician merchants reached Greece, their Greek customers not only bought their wares but adopted their system of notation, changing the phonetic values of some signs and adding others to suit the needs of their own language.

The Greeks, however, retained the Semitic names of the letters they borrowed. As a result, the letter names "alpha" and "beta" (from which our word "alphabet" comes) mean nothing in Greek. Instead, they echo the Phoenician words "aleph" (=ox) and "bet" (=house), recalling the objects the Phoenicians thought their letter shapes resembled. The very word "alphabet" thus echoes the story of its Near Eastern origin.[9]

Greek mythmakers would later say the alphabet was brought to Greece by a Phoenician prince named Cadmus, who came in search of his kidnapped sister. Like the names of the letters, Cadmus's own name turns out to be Semitic, based on a word that meant "the east." Thus Cadmus is the archetypal "man of the east," a legendary symbol for the nameless Phoenician merchants who brought the alphabet to Europe[10] almost three thousand years ago.

The Greek Awakening

Greece's own age of heroes, which reached its climax in the Trojan War, took place long before the Greeks ever learned the alphabet.[11] Their storytellers, however, kept the deeds of their heroes alive in memory in a series of sagas passed on orally from bard to bard, the most famous of whom was a poet called Homer.

The sagas themselves were heroic in proportion. *The Iliad*, the story of the warrior Achilles, contains almost sixteen thousand verses; *The Odyssey*, the story of the wanderer Odysseus, about twelve thousand. As such, Greek epic poetry is a grand testament to memory's power. For centuries the poems provided Greece with moral guidance, long after the heroic world they described had passed.[12] Indeed, it was the image of that earlier world, and the mnemonic ability of poets to keep it alive, that inspired the Greeks to persist in their heroic quest. Soon after the coming of the alphabet, the Homeric poems were set down in writing, but by that time they had already achieved the revered status of scripture.

For the Greeks, the alphabet served other dynamic purposes. Because of its simplicity, it enabled individuals to set down their thoughts and feelings, and through their talent to search for a kind of literary immortality that life itself denied. As the poet Sappho would prophesy in a love poem: "Let me tell you this: someone in some future time will think of us."[13] In personal poems such as this and in plays both tragic and comic the gifted Greeks distilled the essence of what it means to be human. And through the medium of the alphabet, that essence was passed on to later ages.

Because it empowered individual citizens with the ability to read and write, the alphabet energized democracy, a political system the Athenians had only recently invented. Driven by the logical bent of the Greeks and their passion for truth, the alphabet facilitated the writing of the first works of true history—not a Near Eastern annalistic record of merely what happened after what, but a penetrating search for cause and effect in human affairs. Through his research and writing, Herodotus, "the father of history," celebrated the glorious deeds that had made fifth-century Athens free, while Thucydides explored the human weaknesses that eventually brought on its downfall.

In the third century B.C., a great library was built in Alexandria, Egypt, a city that had been founded by Alexander the Great. There Greek scholars gathered to preserve and comment upon the literary heritage of Greek civilization. A royal edict required every ship entering Alexandria's harbor to surrender for copying all books it carried on board. Eventually the library, the first public library in the history of the world, housed as many as five hundred thousand handwritten scrolls, the equivalent of one hundred thousand modern books.[14]

For centuries, the Greek heritage had also been commemorated in visual terms. The legends of the past, with their mythic examples of sacrifice and valor, were made visible in the sculptural decoration of temples in cities across the Greek world. Even for citizens who were illiterate, there were civic lessons clearly to be read in public art.[15] Meanwhile in the countryside outside the cities, families of farmers and herdsmen lived out their lives, performing ancestral rites at altars and recalling days past in story and song.

The arts in Greece—including literature, sculpture, and music—depended upon memory. This was true not only because creative works commemorated the past but also because the creators themselves honored the past by following the footsteps of their teachers.

In Greek mythology, the patrons of the arts were the nine divine Muses, whose mother was Mnemosyne (mnĕ-mó-su-nē), the goddess of memory.[16] Thus memory was regarded as a thing divine from which all creativity sprang. The concept that creativity depended for its existence upon and derived its strength from the remembrance of the past was therefore deeply imbedded in Greek thought.

The Power of Myth

Fiction has the power to move people as much as fact, and ethnic traditions need not be purely factual to rule people's minds and hearts. When the record of actual events is interwoven with imagination, the result is the fabric of myth. Passed down as they are from one generation to another, myths have magical power because they are energized by time. It is by the vital energy that flows from the pole of the past to the pole of the present that a culture's identity and purpose is illuminated. Though such memories are not totally empirical, they are nonetheless wholly human.

To speak of something as a "myth" today implies that it never really happened. Yet what we disparage as mythology, the Greeks and others would have called their hallowed history, no less valid for the distance that separated them from the events their stories described. National myths embody truths that transcend time and as such can shape the future.

The Roman Conquest of Time

Soon after Alexandria's library was built, a new power arose in the world. By the middle of the second century B.C., it had become the political and military master of the Mediterranean. That power was Rome.

When they began their imperialistic expansion, the Romans possessed neither literature nor art. Both, however, were needed if they were to hold their heads high as rulers of the civilized world. To acquire them, they borrowed from the Greeks, but only in ways that were consistent with their own national temperament and aspirations.[17] They thus copied literary genres like epic, history, and rhetoric to proclaim their achievements and destiny.

The Romans were not above stealing someone else's past. To give themselves an heroic pedigree, they claimed Rome had been founded by the descendants of Aeneas, a Trojan prince. To portray their reigns as divinely ordained, Julius and Augustus Caesar traced their lineage to Aeneas and his goddess mother.

The Romans also expropriated the Greek past physically—"requisitioning" priceless statues to adorn their villas, "liberating" private libraries to enrich their shelves, and "engaging" prisoners of war to carve their noble faces in stone. In effect, the Roman conquerors plundered the aesthetic and literary memories of another race.

The Romans, of course, had memories of their own. In the days of the Republic, they looked to their ancestors for ethical instruction and models of patriotic action. As the Latin poet Ennius declared: "On ancient ways and heroes stands the Roman state."[18] The death masks of these same honored ancestors were carried in ritual procession on sacred days. A unique Roman god, Janus, even had two faces, one turned ahead to the future, the other back toward the past.

As Rome's power grew, Republic changed to Empire. During the Empire, more than ever before, Rome's totalitarian leaders used public art to control the minds of the masses.[19] Architectural complexes like the Colosseum and the Baths of Caracalla used carnal entertainment and pleasure to make people forget the political liberties they no longer possessed. On monuments, plastic surgery erased the names and altered the faces of hated political foes. Triumphal arches, towering columns, and propagandistic coins populated a landscape in which all defects and failures were retouched or excised. In the hands of the emperors, memory became as malleable as clay.

Political Death and Spiritual Resurrection

Besides synthesizing the cultural experience of Greece, Roman civilization absorbed the spiritual consciousness of Christianity. When internal weakness and external pressure threatened the stability of the state in the fourth century, the emperor Constantine aligned it with the Church whose enemy and persecutor it had long been.

Recognizing Christianity, however, did not simply mean accepting a set of beliefs; it also meant acquiring new memories. Christianity was rooted in the thought world of the Near East, in the promises of the Old Testament and the revelations of the New. Each testament was, in effect, a contract signed long ago between humanity and God, embodying moral responsibilities and spiritual rewards. The Bible was also an account of human experiences and events dating back hundreds and thousands of years from the creation of life to the lives of the apostles. To acknowledge Christianity as an organized religion was to validate these memories; to accept Christianity as one's personal faith was to accept them as one's own.

This truth is painted on the walls of the catacombs, the communal burial places of Rome's early Christian community.[20] There we see images of Adam and Eve and Moses, of Daniel in the lions' den and Jonah and the whale, of Jesus and his disciples and the miracles their teacher performed.

Often, distant events are viewed through contemporary eyes, as when Hebrew heroes appear in "modern" Roman dress. The painful memory of the crucifixion, still a palpable threat to Christians in Roman days, was suppressed, however, and not portrayed.[21] Elsewhere confusion reigned over whether Jesus was clean-shaven or bearded, since scripture gave no clue.[22] Yet inadequate as it was, memory still remained the spiritual fountain from which the faithful drank.

Ultimately when the Roman Empire in the West fell to the barbarians, it was the Christian church that provided the continuity so necessary to preserve civilization. The Latin language, the language of pagan Rome, became the language of the Catholic Church. The basilica, originally a Roman gathering hall, became the architectural model for places of worship. And during the Dark Ages, when the flame of civilization was nearly extinguished, it was in monasteries that Classical manuscripts were preserved and recopied out of reverence for a lost world.[23] Though long dead, pagan masters like Plato and Aristotle, Cicero and Vergil, arose like ghosts to guide the thinkers of the Middle Ages.

Two noble experiments in education deserve mention. To resist the forces of barbarism, Charlemagne, the Frankish king and Holy Roman Emperor (742–814), founded a palace school to teach the Classics and established schools throughout his empire to instruct children of all social classes. In an England menaced by Danish invaders, King Alfred (848–901) learned Latin at the age of forty so he could supervise the translation of key works on Christian ritual, English history and culture, world history and geography, and moral philosophy. Alfred's intent was "to rebuild the mind of England"[24] and thereby save British civilization. As political leaders in a time of chaos, both Charlemagne and Alfred recognized that a determined national defense would be impossible without cultural memory, for without that memory people would not know what they were fighting for.

Though literacy continued to be limited, by the ninth through twelfth centuries universities offering programs in theology, law, and medicine arose in such cities as Salerno, Bologna, Paris, Oxford, and Cambridge. For scholars, fluency in Latin became the linguistic passport that gave them access to the knowledge and wisdom of the past.[25]

Memory and Rebirth

In the Middle Ages, memorabilia of the Classical Age survived not only in the form of manuscripts but in the form of monuments. This was especially true in Italy, the original homeland of Roman civilization. Despite their ruined state, battered buildings and mutilated statues gave defiant testimony beneath sun and sky to the creative powers that had once belonged to the human spirit. Together they constituted a man-made panorama of memory.

Rather than focusing on this life, medieval thinkers had dwelt on the life to come. In later Italy, however, growing commercial wealth led to intellectual ferment, to an impassioned reconsideration of human possibilities in the here and now. Rich and patriotic city-states like Florence were inspired, in turn, to celebrate their material success in material terms.

> It was under the Medici, or in their day, that the humanists captivated the mind of Italy, turned it from religion to philosophy, from heaven to earth, and revealed to an astonished generation the riches of pagan thought and art. These men mad about scholarship received . . . the name *umanisti* because they called the study of classic culture *umanità*—the humanities—or *literae humaniores*—not "more humane" but more human letters. The proper study of mankind was now to be man, in all the potential strength and beauty of his body, in all the joy and pain of his senses and feelings, in all the frail majesty of his reason; and in these as most abundantly and perfectly revealed in the literature and art of ancient Greece and Rome. This was humanism.[26]

Cities such as Florence might still be proudly Christian, but they were also proud heirs to the humanistic heritage of Classical Italy, to "the glory that was Greece, and the grandeur that was Rome."[27] In consequence, Biblical and Classical traditions blended as never before. Michelangelo might sculpt a Moses, a David, or a Pietà, but his visual inspiration came not from scripture but from the statues, muscular or tender, of a world once lost but now reclaimed. He might design a new basilica in Rome to memorialize Saint Peter, but its dome would give homage to a pagan temple, the Pantheon, to Michelangelo a structure of angelic not human design. If in the "Age of Faith" the angels had stood outside of man, in the "Age of Rebirth," the Renaissance, man discovered his own angelic powers within. Recovered memories had generated creative force.

THE MEMORY REVOLUTION

The Power of the Press

In the fifteenth century, the same century in which Michelangelo was born, a discovery would be made that would revolutionize the preservation and transmission of memory. It would also have a profound effect upon the political and religious history of the Western world. The discovery was typography, the use of movable type on a printing press to make books, and its discoverer was a German, Johann Gutenberg.[28] By making it possible for more people to have more access to more knowledge, Gutenberg changed the world, though he could have hardly imagined it, since he died only twelve years after printing his first work, a copy of the Bible. But change the world he did.

> Before Gutenberg nearly all education had been in the hands of the Church. Books were costly; copying was laborious and sometimes careless. Few authors could reach a wide audience until they were dead; they had to live by pedagogy, or by entering a monastic order, or by pensions from the rich or benefices from the Church. . . .[29]
>
> Printing replaced esoteric manuscripts with inexpensive texts rapidly multiplied, in copies more exact and legible than before, and so uniform that scholars in diverse countries could work with one another by references to specific pages of specific editions. . . . Printing published—i.e., made available to the public—cheap manuals of instruction in religion, literature, history, and science; it became the greatest and cheapest of all universities, open to all. It did not produce the Renaissance, but it paved the way for the Enlightenment, for the American and French revolutions, for democracy. It made the Bible a common possession, and prepared the people for Luther's appeal from the popes to the Gospels; later it would permit the rationalist's appeal from the Gospels to reason. It ended the clerical monopoly of learning, the priestly control of education. It encouraged the vernacular literatures, for the large audience it required could not be reached through Latin. It facilitated the international communication and cooperation of scientists. It affected the quality and character of literature by subjecting authors to the purse and taste of the middle classes rather than to aristocratic or ecclesiastical patrons. And, after speech, it provided a readier instrument for the dissemination of nonsense than the world has ever known until our time.[30]

Gutenberg's invention would have been impossible had it not been for the earlier inventions of writing and the alphabet. Printing's full potential, however, would not be realized until a series of nineteenth-century advances—the steam-powered press, the rotary press, the electric-powered press, and mechanical typesetting—multiplied its speed and output.

The Gutenberg press fed the Renaissance hunger for knowledge, and that greater knowledge led men to challenge the authoritarian power of church and state. As historian Robert Darnton has stated: "The printing press helped shape the events it recorded."[31] In the eighteenth century, incendiary journals and pamphlets ignited revolutions here and in France, fanning flames that later spread across Europe and Latin America.[32] In the democratic systems that arose, public education helped to make basic literacy the common possession of all citizens. Eventually in 1791, the Gutenberg legacy was enshrined in the First Amendment of America's Bill of Rights.

Thus a machine wrought a revolution by giving Western civilization unprecedented access to the liberating ideas and experiences of earlier generations.

The Artificial Brain

In a sense, every culture has a brain, which grows in response to the complexity of the culture's life.[33] A culture must have a place for the storage of experience, a medium onto which experience is transcribed: the prehistoric wall, the cuneiform tablet, the papyrus scroll, the medieval manuscript, the printed page. A culture must also have a place where these experiences are housed and protected: the cave, the temple, the monastery, the library—the cultural equivalent of the skull. And it must also have a system by which past experience can be transmitted: the oral tradition of bards, the mechanics of literacy, a system of schools. As a culture becomes more populous and the lives of its inhabitants more intertwined, new inventions (writing, the alphabet, the printing press) arise to enable it to communicate with itself more efficiently and to integrate new experience more rapidly with old in order to survive as an organism in a changing environment.

In the nineteenth and twentieth centuries, further technological advances—the telegraph, the telephone, radio, and television—have made possible the transmission of information across vast distances at the speed of light, while other inventions—the phonograph, the camera, and the video recorder—have captured and preserved experience. Among the newest of these innovations is the computer, offering unprecedented personal access to incredible stores of knowledge. Of all modern devices, the computer comes closest to the human brain in its amazingly compact storage capacity, its electrical operation, and its instantaneous response. But, so far at least, the computer lacks consciousness.[34] It has "memory but not remembrance."[35]

All the while, the computer tells us we know so much. It seductively comforts us with the intimacy of its keys and the data they put at our touch. Yet behind us, looking over our shoulder, stands Pharaoh Thamus, contemplating this latest gift of Thoth and wondering if, by our dependency, we may ultimately lose more than we gain.[36] "You give your disciples," he whispers, "only the pretense of wisdom; they will be hearers of many things but will have understood nothing."

CHAPTER 4

THE POWER OF
OBLIVION

If the history of civilization is the history of remembrance, it is also the story of forgetting.

In the individual mind, as we have seen, the loss of memories is as natural as their retention: some transient experiences leave no imprint on our consciousness; the impression of others lasts only for a short while, like lines from a story casually read; still others occupy a more permanent place on the bookshelves of our mind, to be taken down and browsed through again and again. But there are other memories, painful ones, that our mind tries to dispose of because of the anguish they cause. Indeed, it may be argued that our psychological survival and health depend upon such acts of voluntary or subconscious renunciation.

THE VANISHING PAST

Nature's Memory

Nature has its own memory. Unlike the human brain, Nature's memory is not encoded in electrochemical form. Instead, its inorganic changes are inscribed in soil and rocks; its organic changes, in fossilized remains and the molecular signature of DNA. Through cellular memory, generations that once populated the past live on in the present, reincarnated by reproduction and heredity.

But if nature has the capacity to remember, it also possesses the power to forget. Rock weathers; soil erodes; vegetation decays; and flesh, once pulsing, rots. Though the biological type may persist, the individual organism perishes, ashes to ashes, dust to dust. In like manner, the works of humanity crumble into ruin.

In the spiritual geography of ancient Greece, the land of the dead was called the kingdom of Hades. In it flowed a river called Lethe (lē-thē), the river of forgetfulness, from which all those who died had to drink.[1] To the Greeks, forgetfulness was an inescapable curse, the daughter of a goddess who brought humanity nothing but strife.[2] Yet if to die was to forget totally, to live fully was to remember.

When Nature first became conscious of itself through evolution, one of its first biologic acts was to remember its past. Its most recent progeny were self-aware creatures called humans among whom art and literature arose as instruments of remembrance to protect and preserve communal experience and individual identity. In time, the human race compiled annals and composed histories to commemorate past events. Later, it invented sciences such as geology (the study of the earth's story), paleontology (the study of early living things), and archaeology (the study of ancient cultures) to explore bygone eras still further.

But the currents of Lethe are swift and voracious.

Disappearing Evidence

Our perception of history is based upon the illusion that the most important facts about the past are known; yet nothing could be further from the truth.

The Stone Age represents the longest epoch of our planetary existence, but it is paradoxically the one about which we know the least, for its narrative is written not in words but in empty skulls. Tens of thousands of generations of men and women were born in prehistoric times and died, only to vanish into oblivion along with their desires and dreams.

Civilization, on the other hand, chronicled itself in inscriptions and monuments. But these testaments were left behind by a small and privileged class that had the requisite wealth and power to mark their status and accomplishments. As to the meek, blessed in the Sermon on the Mount, they inherited the earth they were buried in, but little else. As a consequence, our eyes behold the glittering splendor of kings but are blind to the anonymous poverty of the masses they ruled.

Yet even literacy is no guarantee against oblivion. Egypt may keep its ancient scrolls secure in its sands, but most of their wisdom is still hidden by that self-same desert. Iraq may hoard its clay tablets in its deserted mounds, but only 1 percent of them has ever been unearthed.[3] Meanwhile, written in cryptic signs and forgotten tongues, the dust-covered biographies of other kingdoms lie eternally unread.[4]

The classic works of Western civilization are themselves but remnants. Sophocles, the profound playwright who wrote *Oedipus Rex*, authored more than 120 tragedies, yet the scripts of only seven survive. Of Greek art, we have temples that are mostly mutilated, vases that are mostly smashed, and statues that are mostly copies. In fact, not a single undisputedly original sculpture survives from the hand of a sculptor whom the Greeks regarded as first-rate.[5]

The Romans were monumental egotists, but their egotism has long since been cut down to size. Though it continues to awe us today, the Colosseum is but a shadow of its former self: only one-third of its mass still remains. And although Vesuvius made Pompeii and Herculaneum time capsules of daily life, other Roman cities died a slower death that left barely enough material for an obituary.[6]

Of the Seven Wonders of the Greco-Roman world, only one—Giza's Great Pyramid—endures, its exterior skin of shimmering limestone long since peeled away, its interior gutted of golden treasure.[7]

Nor have we spoken of the things the ancients did not display but instead kept deliberately hidden, the long-lost secrets that their priests and engineers took with them to the grave. Indeed, even the raw materials used by the people of antiquity to depict themselves—cold and unyielding stone and cool bronze—obscure a larger truth: the vibrancy and humanity of their inner lives.

Where the people of the past scrawled their signature, it has been erased by natural processes. The rushing and seepage of water, the crushing growth of vegetation, the shock of earthquakes, and the feasting of termites have conspired to destroy the vestiges of earlier times. As the planet's population has risen, its monuments have been invaded by multitudes hungry for more land to build on and more resources to exploit. Industrialization has released chemical pathogens into the air responsible for not only maladies of the body but also for ills infecting statues: marble "cancer" and corrosive bronze "disease." In consequence, decade-old slides shown in art history classes reveal details on sculpture and architecture that have vanished forever and will never return.

Oscar Wilde once wrote that "all men kill the thing they love."[8] Translated into tourism, such love has led to the desecration of sites by graffiti and their pilferage for souvenirs. Even the touch of the human hand with its oily residue, the tread of feet too close to fragile ground, the rise in temperature from the nearness of the human body, and the exhalation of moisture and carbon dioxide from the lungs can hasten the deterioration of what is already old. Compounding these effects is the acrid exhaust of the planes and tour buses that bring eager hordes of camera-toting tourists to their daily destinations.

Some countries have suspended the further excavation of known archaeological sites so that precious dollars can be spent on preserving what has already been found rather than subjecting new discoveries to above-ground risks.[9] Other countries have removed monuments from their original sites, setting up replicas in their place.[10] The traveler is therefore well advised to see the world before it goes away, leaving behind only a Disneyesque facsimile of its former self.

With increasing frequency, the love of art has inspired looting by individual entrepreneurs and organized crime rings, especially in countries too poor to protect their national treasures adequately from the greed of their own countrymen and the appetite of foreign collectors.[11] The looting of art, of course, is a story as old as antiquity itself. In modern times, archaeology began with Europeans "liberating" artworks from their east Mediterranean homelands until the rise of nationalism in such countries put an end to the practice.[12] Today, international negotiations drag on for the repatriation of these treasures against the resistance of the Western museums that still house them.[13]

Paradoxically, even attempts to restore old works of art have contributed to their destruction. The road to curatorial hell is paved not only with good aesthetic intentions but also with inadequately tested detergents, solvents, and glues that have often caused irreparable harm to the very works they were meant to restore.[14]

In addition to endangered species, our planet also has endangered sites. Currently, 440 places of historic importance are in peril according to UNESCO's World Heritage Center in Paris.[15] World Monuments Watch, a private organization, lists one hundred as savable if enough money and civic will can be marshalled.[16] For many countries, however, the total budget for preserving all of their historic sites is barely enough to save even one. As Italian archaeologist Giovanni Scichilone has complained: "Our national patrimony . . . is living a slow and frightening agony."[17]

A prime example of an endangered monument is India's Taj Mahal, erected in the seventeenth century by an emperor as a tribute to his deceased wife and ever since a symbol of beauty and love. Today, instead of being embraced by love, the Taj is gripped by pollution. Thousands of sulfur-producing coal-burning factories and diesel-powered generating plants surround it in a noxious ring, while India's biggest oil refinery hovers nearby, spewing a ton of sulfur dioxide into the air every hour. The chemical consequence of all these fumes is the staining and eating away of the Taj Mahal's skin, yet India's Archaeological Survey is almost powerless to intervene: besides guarding the Taj Mahal, it has been responsible for protecting three thousand other monuments with a total budget of only $65,000.[18]

In the United States over a decade ago, a special effort was undertaken to save an exceptional American monument, the Statue of Liberty. Repairing Lady Liberty's cracked and corroded skin and reinforcing her wrought-iron skeleton cost millions of dollars and two years of constant work. The scaffolding was finally removed, and on July 4, 1986—her one hundredth birthday—the statue's flame was once again lit.[19]

But the Statue of Liberty is an exception. As Stewart L. Udall points out: "In the United States, laws protect archaeological sites on public lands. However, *most* sites are located on private lands, where they are *not* protected. That means property owners control the fate of many of America's most important prehistoric and historic sites. As a result, most sites simply disappear: bulldozed, leveled, [or] looted."[20]

Even monuments on public land are not safe. In New York City's thousand parks there are some fifteen hundred public monuments, over half of which have major sculptural or architectural features, most of which are degenerating into what preservationist Donald Martin Reynolds has termed "Monuments to Neglect."[21]

In addition, the National Park Service already has a $1 billion backlog of projects to restore historic sites that each day deteriorate more and more.[22] Among them is Thomas Alva Edison's marvelous "Invention Laboratory," housing four hundred thousand precious artifacts and five million personal documents, including laboratory notes and letters, many of which are even now crumbling.[23]

Yet besides the immediate causes that are destroying the historic remains of the past, there are deeper and more intractable ones.

First of all, there is human nature itself. Sexual desire impels propagation which, in turn, drives the growth of population and cities that have overrun former sanctuaries of historic memory. The economic needs and material desires people feel in the present readily take precedence over the claims of a dead or dying past. Thus, building a new subdivision makes more sense than preserving an old cemetery, and getting a new shopping mall counts for more than keeping a deserted battlefield.

Coupled with Nature's destructive bent, there is mankind's own. It is far easier to destroy than to create, and mankind has vented his individual and collective fury in destructive acts since the dawn of history, acts of demonic self-expression that have not only taken life but erased the remnants of that life as well. Apart from the annihilation caused by war, there are pernicious acts of vandalism that regularly rob us of our past. The gradual deterioration of monuments rather than their sudden destruction is a process so slow that it is invisible to the eye until years have passed and dramatic before-and-after photographs are examined. Nor is the year-in-year-out maintenance of monuments an exciting enough prospect to inspire much public or private support.

More potent than anything else, however, is the inexorable passage of time that not only causes monuments to deteriorate but also psychologically and culturally distances our sensibilities from their intrinsic significance, exempting acts of neglect and destruction from the purview of our personal and social conscience. Indeed, as fewer and fewer traces of the past persist, there is less and less incentive to remember or value what once was.

But it is not grand monuments alone that are in danger; the records of daily life are in peril as well. Although our era has been dubbed the Information Age, that very information is startlingly subject to decay either because of the fragility of the material on which it is inscribed or the rapid obsolescence of the technology needed to understand it. According to UNESCO, "three-quarters of the films which were made worldwide before 1950 have already disappeared."[24] The average life expectancy of magnetic tapes, both audio and video, is only about ten years; of optical disks, fifty; of archival-quality microfilm, only a hundred. In fact, after only five years, average-quality CD-ROMs are either unreadable or unreliable.[25]

Part of the problem is that tapes and disks, unlike paper, often do not show degradation until it's too late. Occasionally tapes become so brittle that the magnetic coating actually separates from its backing. More often, however, the signs of damage are subtle: Routine exposure to magnetic fields will rearrange some of the tape's magnetized iron particles. When a machine plays the degraded tapes, these alterations make the tapes unreadable, resulting in missing data. A few years ago, for example, scientists from NASA's Jet Propulsion Laboratory tried to read some of the magnetic tapes that contained the results of the 1976 Viking mission to Mars—tapes that had been carefully stored and appeared to be in good shape. [But] 10 to 20 percent of them had missing data. . . .

Even more troubling than the fragility of storage media, however, is how rapidly computer hardware and software become obsolete. Unlike paper documents and traditional audio and video recordings—which as analog media present a continuous, start-to-finish record of information—computers store data digitally. By breaking information into electronic or magnetic strings of 1s and 0s, digital technology has made it possible to store and access enormous volumes of data using very little space. But without the programs and equipment used to encode it, digital information makes no sense.[26]

Referring to the immortality of a printed poem, Shakespeare's eighteenth sonnet once ended with the following couplet "So long as men can breathe or eyes can see / So long lives this and this gives life to thee." But according to Jeff Rothenberg, a senior computer scientist at the Rand Corporation, Shakespeare would need to revise his verses if he were talking about a digitally stored poem:

So long as the magnetic flux on this disk has not been disturbed, and so long as humans retain the appropriate size and speed disk drives, and so long as they have hardware controllers and software device drivers capable of reading the bits from this disk, and so long as they have access to the software that encoded the file structure and character codes employed in the bit stream of this document, and so long as they can still find or recreate the computing environment necessary to run that software, *and* so long as they can still breathe or see / So long lives this and this gives life to thee.[27]

Referring to the World Wide Web, Microsoft executive Nathan Myhrvold warns how Internet data will likewise disappear unless deliberate efforts are made to preserve it.

The Web is losing its history. . . . Every day the Web becomes more and more important in academics, business and ultimately contemporary culture itself. The surprising truth is that the early days of the digital age will appear almost pre-literate to future historians. Sure, we were all writing, but if we don't save it, it isn't part of the historical record.

The hype about the Web is better archived (in libraries, etc.) than the Web itself. Do we want the Web to be remembered by that?[28]

According to Stewart Brand, creator of the *Whole Earth Catalog*, "There has never been a time of such drastic and irretrievable information loss. . . . We've turned into a total amnesiac. We do short-term memory, period."[29]

Ironically, it is old-fashioned paper that is the most durable memory sponge.[30] Low-acid paper can last a century; when buffered, half a millennium.[31] Yet it is paper that our electronic society is progressively moving away from at the speed of light. Rather than being named the Information Age, our times might better be dubbed the "Age of Impermanence."

The Power of Now

The latest, however, and least recognized threat to the preservation of the past resides in the very nature of our electronic media, which thrive on the moment and on the new. Indeed, the "power of now," "the intense energy of an unconditional present, a present uncompromised by any other dimension of time"[32] suffuses our popular culture, crowding out whatever space was formerly reserved for the remembrance of things past. As our society accelerates under the influence of speed-of-light technologies, the past recedes from our consciousness. Of all the causes of oblivion, the power of now is the most insidious, because it steals our cultural memories while simultaneously gratifying us with excitement and pleasure.

THE PAIN OF REMEMBRANCE

More than blood, it is memory that confers identity on an ethnic group and sustains its life. Without the remembrance of a common homeland and ancestry, without the recollection of shared suffering and joy, a group lacks the coherence needed to maintain its integrity as it journeys through time. In the historic hearth-fire of memory a people's soul is warmed; in the fire's flickering light are glimpses of its uniqueness and purpose. But sparks from that selfsame fire can also ignite the flames of conflagration: when people recall the pain inflicted upon them in the past by others whose wrongful acts have never been punished, a desire for revenge can arise.

Memory's Scars

About fifty miles south of Baghdad near the banks of the Euphrates lie the ruins of Babylon, once the capital of an ancient empire. In the sixth century B.C., Nebuchadnezzar, the Babylonian king, invaded and conquered the Biblical land of Judah and destroyed Jerusalem, its holy capital. To weaken his enemy and insure their compliance to his will, Nebuchadnezzar took ten thousand Judaeans prisoner and deported them to Babylon to be slaves and hostages. While there, a nameless Hebrew poet recalled his beloved city and its temple, and prayed for return. His poem survives in the Bible as the 137th Psalm.

> By the waters of Babylon, there we sat down and wept,
>   when we remembered Zion.
> On the willows there
>   we hung up our lyres.
> For there our captors
>   required of us songs,
> and our tormentors, mirth, saying,
>   "Sing us one of the songs of Zion!"
> How shall we sing the Lord's song
>   in a foreign land?
> If I forget you, O Jerusalem,
>   let my right hand wither!
> Let my tongue cleave to the roof of my mouth,
>   If I do not remember you,
> If I do not set Jerusalem
>   above my highest joy!

In the next stanza, however, the poet—mindful of the brutality inflicted on his people—prays to God for revenge. Indeed, he asks God himself to remember history.

> Remember, O Lord, against the Edomites
>   the day of Jerusalem,
> how they said "Rase it, rase it!
>   Down to its foundations!"

> O daughter of Babylon, you devastator!
>   Happy shall be he who requites you with what you have done to us!
> Happy shall be he who takes your little ones
>   and dashes them against the rock![33]

The paradox of memory, then, is that it can inspire a people with both love and hate. Feeding upon the pain of the past, an ethnic group can yearn for revenge against its enemies.

Perhaps more than love, hate can clarify complexity and focus emotion; it can galvanize a multitude with the energy of a single, overpowering idea. Under the right circumstances and conditions, the historical desire for revenge, pent up for ages, can be unleashed with terrifying fury.

In the concluding decades of the twentieth century, the world witnessed a firestorm of ethnic conflicts fueled by memory. In some cases these conflicts stemmed from competing claims to ancestral territory; in others, from a clash of religious tradition; and in still others from both. Usually, the protagonists were, on the one hand, a minority that sought political self-determination and, on the other, a majority that sought to suppress that right. Like memory itself, many of these struggles persist to this day, and in succeeding years others, no doubt, will be added to a globally inclusive list already far too long. Here, in alphabetical order, are some of the conflicts of the 1980s and 1990s.[34]

Afghanistan (Hazars vs. Pathans vs. Tajiks)

Algeria (Islamic militants vs. the Government)

Angola (Savimbi guerillas vs. the Government; Cabinda secessionists vs. the Government)

Azerbaijan (Christian Armenians vs. the Muslim-dominated Government; Kurdish separatists vs. the Government)

Bangladesh (Buddhist Chakmas vs. the Muslim majority)

Bhutan (ethnic Nepalese vs. the Government)

Bosnia and Herzegovina (Serbs vs. Muslims and Croats)

Brazil (Amazonian tribes vs. the Government; the Government vs. gold miners in tribal lands)

Britain (Protestants vs. Catholics in Northern Ireland; whites vs. Asian immigrants and blacks)

Burundi (majority Hutus vs. minority Tutsis)

Cambodia (rebel factions vs. the Government; Khmer Rouge soldiers vs. ethnic Vietnamese)

Chad (rebellions involving the Zakawa tribe vs. the Gourane tribe)

China (Tibetans vs. the Government; Turkic Muslims vs. the Government)

Colombia (Indian insurgents vs. the Government; Marxist guerillas vs. the Government)

Croatia (Serbian separatists vs. the Government)

Egypt (Islamic militants vs. the Government; Islamic militants vs. Coptic Christians)

Fiji (ethnic Fijis vs. the Indian-dominated Government)

Georgia (Muslim separatists vs. the Government)

Germany (right-wing and neo-Nazi groups vs. asylum seekers from Bulgaria, Romania, the Balkans, and other areas)

Guatemala (leftist guerillas vs. the Government; Indians vs. the Government)

India (Hindus vs. Muslims; Kashmiri militants vs. the Government; Punjabi Hindus vs. Punjabi Sikhs; Assam secessionists vs. the Government; Nagaland separatists vs. the Government)

Indonesia (Roman Catholic East Timorese vs. the Government; Sumatra separatists vs. the Government)

Iraq (Kurds vs. the Government; Shiite Muslims vs. the Sunni-Muslim-dominated Government)

Israel (Palestinians vs. Israelis)

Kenya (tribal clashes, perhaps incited by the Government to deter democracy)

Liberia (Gio and Mano ethnic groups vs. the ethnically Krahn Government)

Mali (ethnic Tuaregs vs. the Government)

Mauritania (the black minority vs. the Arab-dominated Government)

Moldova (ethnic Russians and Ukrainians vs. ethnic Romanians)

Myanamar (Muslims vs. the Government; clashes between Burmese soldiers and separatist Karen and other insurgents on the Thai-Burmese border)

Niger (Tuaregas vs. the Government)

Nigeria (Muslim Hausas vs. mostly Christian Yorubas)

Pakistan (clashes between the Government and insurgents in Sindh and the Northwest Frontier Province; rioting in Karachi involving ethnically Indian Muslims)

Papua New Guinea (Bougainville rebels vs. the Government)

Peru (Maoist guerillas supported by Indian and mixed-race groups vs. the Hispanic-controlled Government)

Romania (ethnic Hungarians vs. the Government; attacks on Gypsies)

Russia (Chechnyan, Ingushetian, and Dagestani rebels vs. the Government; territorial clashes between Ingushetia and Northern Ossetia)

Rwanda (minority Tutsi invaders vs. majority Hutu Government)

Senegal (Diola minority vs. Muslim-dominated Government)

Serbia (ethnic Albanian rebels vs. the Government)

Somalia (clan fighting and civil war)

South Africa (black insurgents vs. the white Government; Zulus vs. rival black groups)

Spain (Basque separatists vs. the Government)

Sri Lanka (Hindu Tamil insurgents vs. the Buddhist-dominated Government; Sinhalese militants vs. the Government)

Sudan (black Christian and animist insurgents vs. the Arab Muslim-dominated Government)

Tajikistan (Tajik Muslims vs. resurgent Communist forces)

Togo (Ewe tribesmen vs. the Government dominated by the Kabiye tribe)

Turkey (Kurdish separatists vs. the Government)

Uganda (civil war between rival tribes)

Yugoslavia (Serb-dominated Government vs. ethnic Albanians in Kosovo Province)

Zaire (civil war involving competing ethnic groups and tribes)

The role of memory in such a deadly litany is a powerful argument for its erasure. A world oblivious to the past would be a safer world, for people would have forgotten their ancestral aspirations and historic grievances and could finally live in peace.

A convincing argument, perhaps—at least until we confront its corollary: that a lobotomized culture is a culture without direction or will, for to excise a people's sense of the past is to rob them of their future as well.[35] Nor is such radical surgery required.

Centuries after the Babylonian Exile, rabbis reflected upon the suffering their people had endured at the hands of oppressors.[36] Before the days of Nebuchadnezzar, another ruler—a pharaoh—had been their enemy. Moses led the Israelites to freedom, but not before the Egyptian army pursued them into the Red Sea and drowned in its waters. Seeing their pursuers dead, Moses and his people sang a song praising God.[37] As the rabbis later told the tale:

> When the Egyptian hosts were drowning in the Red Sea, the angels in heaven were about to break forth into songs of jubilation. But the Holy one, blessed be He, silenced them with the words, "My creatures are perishing, and ye are ready to sing!" In the same spirit, a medieval rabbi explained why a drop of wine is poured out of the wine-cup on [Passover] Seder eve at the mention of each of the plagues that were inflicted on the Egyptians. Israel's cup of joy, he said, cannot be full if Israel's triumph involves suffering even to its enemies.[38]

According to such tradition, then, ethnic persecution need not require vengeance nor preclude the forgiveness of one's enemies. What is needed is time. For the Hebrew poet sitting by the waters of Babylon, not enough time had passed for the wounds of hate to heal. For later generations, however, that time would come. In the words of the post-Exilic book of Ecclesiastes:

> For everything there is a season,
> and a time for every matter under heaven:
> a time to be born, and a time to die;
> a time to plant, and a time to pluck up what is planted;
> a time to kill, and a time to heal;
> a time to break down, and a time to build up;
> a time to weep, and a time to laugh;
> a time to mourn, and a time to dance;
> a time to cast away stones, and a time to gather stones together;
> a time to embrace, and a time to refrain from embracing;
> a time to seek, and a time to lose;
> a time to keep, and a time to cast away;
> a time to rend, and a time to sew;
> a time to keep silence, and a time to speak;
> a time to love, and a time to hate;
> a time for war, and a time for peace.[39]

To which we may add: "a time to remember, and a time to forget."

Yet if God's angels could not resist exulting over fallen enemies, it may be too much to expect better behavior from mere mortals. Nevertheless, if human beings are ever to live in peace, they must gain rational control over their impulses. To do so does not necessarily mean to forget; rather, it means to remember in a different way.

The Jews of modern Israel have not forgotten the wounds of the Holocaust. Many still carry the searing scars with them every day, their concentration-camp numbers tattooed on both skin and memory. To forget loved ones lost would be to desecrate their lives, to murder them once again. Indeed, once a year in Israel, sirens wail and all work and traffic stops as people pause to remember.[40] "Never again" is memory's cry, for remembrance is also a defense against the repetition of evil.[41]

Indeed, through thousands of years of persecution the memory of past suffering has bonded Jews together and has helped them survive as a people. As Elie Wiesel has said: "Memories, even painful memories, are all we have. In fact, they are the only thing we are."[42] But remembrance cannot be synonymous with hate else victims become one with the haters who wish them dead.

For Israelis, it is easier to make peace with yesterday's enemies than today's: Palestinian enemies who share the same land, whose ancestral claims are as strong, whose humanity is as non-negotiable. In contemporary Israeli-Palestinian politics, cool detachment is not an option; instead, it is from memory's boiling crucible that the future will be poured. Yet hope remains.

Reporter David K. Shipler, former Jerusalem bureau chief for the *New York Times*, recalls a moving experience "when 16 Jewish-American and Palestinian-American women, leaders of Jewish and Arab organizations who had been holding dialogues for several years, visited Israel and the occupied territories together."[43]

> The schedule called for a day trip to Gaza followed by a visit to Yad Vashem, the Holocaust museum in Jerusalem. Several Palestinians did not wish to see Yad Vashem, arguing that they already knew about the Holocaust, that they weren't responsible for it, and that it had been used as a tool against them, according to Reena Bernards, one of the group's coordinators.
>
> One Palestinian woman insisted that the horrible images would disturb her sleep, and she refused to put herself through the experience.

The Jewish women were upset, and Yad Vashem stayed on the agenda, with everyone free to go or not as she chose.

In Gaza, the women were guided through the twisting alleys of the Beach Refugee Camp to a three-room house with a concrete floor, home to a family of 17. In one room, where seven people slept, bedding was carefully folded each morning and placed in the closet.

"People were very moved by the whole experience in Gaza," Ms. Bernards recalls, and the Palestinian women were touched by Jews' willingness to go out of their way to see suffering.

Everyone was asked to write her reflections briefly, then read them aloud to the group that evening. A politically conservative Jewish woman expressed her compassion for the Gazans living in squalor who neatly folded their bedding as a way to maintain their dignity. She said no one should have to live like that.

The last to speak was the Palestinian who had not wanted to lose sleep over the images in the Holocaust museum. Ms. Bernards remembers her brief statement: "The only thing I want to say is that I will go to Yad Vashem." And she did, along with the others.[44]

The bridge of reconciliation between contending ethnic groups may in fact rest upon such realizations as this: the recognition that both sides are brothers and sisters by virtue of the common suffering they have separately known. If so, memory may ultimately humanize and heal just as once it hurt.[45]

Yet is it possible to keep one part of our memory alive while suppressing another? Or are the light and the darkness trapped in our synapses inevitably paired?

The answers to these questions will define the future of our race even as they have already shaped its past. To succeed as a humane culture, we must consciously choose what is right to remember and what is better to forget, for only by tenaciously holding on to one and freely letting go of the other can we find our common salvation. As philosopher Charles Morris once wrote: "The dark powers of the night are in ourselves. But also in ourselves are the powers that can carry us into the dawn."[46]

Assassins of Memory

Victims do not have an irrevocable claim to memory. Oppressors can not only ravage the present but can also rob survivors of their past. As history shows, "ethnic cleansing"[47] can mean not only the deportation and execution of persons but also the extermination of their tradition.

Because books are the reservoirs of remembrance, it is books and those knowledgeable in them that enemies target. In the 1960s Mao Tse-tung's Red Guard subjected professors to physical abuse because, as guardians of the past, scholars were deemed enemies of progress. In the same way, the Emperor Chin, who built China's Great Wall, had marched Confucian scholars to forced labor camps over two thousand years before.[48] Today, in Chinese-controlled Tibet, possessing a book by the Dalai Lama can similarly result in years of imprisonment.[49] Chin also initiated the public burning of "dangerous" books, a practice later carried out by sixteenth-century Spanish priests in the lands of the Maya and by twentieth-century Jew-hating Nazis in Germany. More recently in Sarajevo, whole libraries were targeted for destruction by Serb gunners, "the largest single incident of book burning in history."[50] According to Enes Kujundžić, director of the National and University Library of Bosnia-Herzegovina, the Serb forces "knew that if they wanted to destroy this multi-ethnic society, they would have to destroy the library. . . . First you destroy the documents, then you quickly destroy the memory that they ever existed."[51] As correspondent Roger Cohen adds: "The target of such acts, of course, is not the monuments alone, but civilization itself. For morality, learning, art, and measure are all embodied in what has fallen."[52]

Perhaps more vulnerable than books are the oral traditions of cultures that lack writing. As historian Kenneth C. Davis points out; "Ethnic cleansing didn't start in Bosnia."[53]

> Virtually absent from the discussion is any acknowledgment that when it comes to the sorts of horrors now defining the Balkan conflict, Americans have been there and done that, in a manner of speaking. To put it bluntly: The United States may not have written the book on ethnic cleansing, but it certainly provided several of its most stunning chapters—particularly in its treatment of the American Indian in the transcontinental drive for territory justified under the quasi-religious notion of "manifest destiny."
>
> Why do we tend to forget? There's no big surprise: Americans, as de Tocqueville long ago recognized, are a future-oriented people with a short historical memory. And the accepted, widely taught versions of history are written by the victors, presented in schools as sanitized costume pageantry. This is especially true when the victory is as total

as that of America's forefathers over the American Indians, who were nearly "cleansed" from an entire continent—an outcome the likes of which Bosnia's Serbs can only dream.[54]

Only in recent decades have Native Americans in the United States and Canada aggressively sought to protect and proudly transmit their oral traditions, and transmute them into writing, creating new works in the process. As author Joseph Bruchac has written: "The gift is still being given."[55]

In the early eighteenth century, it was proposed by serious scholars that Native Americans lacked real languages and were only questionably human. A century and a half ago, people still questioned the existence of literary traditions (or, quite frankly, any real culture) among the Native peoples of North America. The vast body of Native American oral traditions now being diligently studied by scholars around the world was either unknown or ignored. A generation of ethnologists, some of them (like Tuscarora J.N.B. Hewitt) Native Americans themselves, made considerable strides in recording and celebrating those oral traditions by the early part of the twentieth century. By then, however, the continued survival of native American people and any aspect of their cultures was being seriously doubted. Genocidal policies of warfare and forced migration, the destruction of means of traditional subsistence (such as the buffalo in the western plains), the outlawing of Native American religious practices, and the continuing epidemics for which native populations had no resistance, seemed to spell the end. The image of the "Vanishing Redman" became a common theme in North American popular culture and still remains prominent in cinematic depictions of Indians.

Yet, despite it all, Native American people survived. . . .

In a world of questions, Native American literature offers answers—not easy solutions, but ones charged with power.[56]

Just as Native Americans were driven from their ancestral lands, so Black Americans were torn from their African roots by the slave trade and—like native American peoples—are today striving to rediscover their history.

One of the most remarkable efforts in this cause has involved the creation of a new holiday, Kwanzaa, now celebrated around the world by people of African descent. The seven-day holiday was invented in 1966 by political scientist Maulana Karenga to unite the black community. Each day of Kwanzaa celebrates a different principle evident in the historical experience of Africans. Named in Swahili, the most common African language, the principles are *umoja* (unity), *kuchichagulia* (self-determination), *ujima* (collective work and responsibility), *ujamaa* (cooperative economics), *nia* (purpose), *kuumba* (creativity), and *imani* (faith). The name of the holiday itself, Kwanzaa (first), refers to the first harvest of the year, a time of traditional rejoicing among African peoples.[57]

The spirit of renewal that underlies the celebration of Kwanzaa is also found in the word *sankofa*, found in the Akan language of central Ghana.

Sankofa . . . roughly translates as "remembering your past in order to move into the future." In other words, the past should serve as guide to our future. It admonishes us not to forget our history and our roots in our current endeavor and undertakings if we are to succeed in the future.[58]

As the words *kwanzaa* and *sankofa* teach us, roots can be found by re-learning the spiritual vocabulary of another time.

The oral testimony to that past can also be preserved with the help of electronic technology. Though a day will soon come when most living witnesses to the Holocaust will have died (there are now about three hundred thousand worldwide, most in their seventies and eighties), their spoken words will endure thanks to the vision, determination, and generosity of Hollywood director, Steven Spielberg.[59] Spielberg's aim is to record the testimony of seventy-five thousand survivors in two-hour videotaped interviews, often filmed in their homes. Enhanced by personal photographs and documents and stored in a computerized database, the interviews will constitute a carefully preserved digital archive for the use of future generations. Named "Shoah," after the Hebrew word for Holocaust, the project will not only rescue the past from oblivion but also challenge the revisionist view that the Holocaust never happened. The recollections of eyewitnesses can be flawed,[60] but such revisionism—the cunning assertion that memory is a deliberate lie—is hatred's ultimate obscenity.[61]

MANIPULATING THE PAST

The manipulation of the past to serve a racial or political agenda has a long history, as old as the propagandistic art of ancient Egypt[62] and Rome.[63] In the twentieth century, Soviet authorities edited history books and retouched old photographs, deleting the names and images of political figures who had fallen out of favor.[64] For the sake of national pride, post-World War II Japanese authorities censored schoolbook accounts of the 1937 rape of Nanking.[65] Similarly, the German public anesthetized its conscience for decades rather than take moral responsibility for the "final solution."[66] Even archaeology has been enlisted in the cause of propaganda, especially in the Middle East, where twentieth-century regimes have twisted archaeological evidence to bolster their nationalistic ambitions.[67]

Like an individual, a nation can rearrange the pieces of the past in order to create a version of the truth that is more psychologically satisfying. And if certain pieces do not fit, a political regime or even a whole people can dispense with them altogether, choosing sweet oblivion over the pain of remembrance. As we will see in the next chapter, drinking from the waters of Lethe can, in fact, become a way of life.

CHAPTER 5

WHY AMERICA
FORGOT

The parade lasted only forty minutes. Only two bands showed up out of four that were invited. Only two companies donated money out of four hundred that were asked. Even the mayor came late.

Some of the marchers moved in wheelchairs, but the few passersby on the sidewalk hardly noticed. The parade seemed to catch them by surprise.

It was Veterans Day, 1996, in New York City.[1]

Ask students in school why Veterans Day falls on November 11. You'll be lucky if anyone has a clue. "Wasn't it the start of the war?" says one student. "Which war?" the teacher asks, and is answered by a shrug. "World War II?" guesses another.

Comments a reporter who covered the parade: "Not too many New Yorkers—or too many Americans, for that matter—care a great deal about veterans or their sacrifices, which were long ago and far away."[2] A Korean War veteran who took part in the march agrees. "It's all ancient history to most people," he says. "It hurts a little bit, but not much. We're used to it."[3]

"What if they had a war and nobody came?" the joke used to go. "What if they had a parade and no one cared?" we could add.

Maybe it was the cold November day that explains the scant turnout, or the early morning hour. Or maybe it was all about something too "long ago and far away." Maybe to most people it was just "ancient history."

On November 11, 1917, the armistice that ended the first (but not the last) global war in human history was signed. Why do so few people remember? And why are they oblivious to so much else about history, even when events took place only a few years ago? In short, why did America forget? That is the subject we will explore.

Our exploration will reveal a number of causes. Significantly, many of them have very little to do with our educational system, but everything to do with the nature of our culture, with the kind of civilization America is and has become.

The long passage of time, the urgent call of the senses, the accelerating power of technology, the lure of materialism, and the newness of our nation have all collaborated in obscuring the past and its meaning. Together, in recent decades, they have also undermined the importance of history and the value of remembering, inducing a state of cultural amnesia in the American mind.

THE CAUSES OF OUR AMNESIA

The Long Passage of Time

Time is the engine of forgetfulness.

As time passes, the distance grows between us and the experiences we have had. And the farther we get from events, the harder they are to recall. Like objects seen in the rearview mirror of a car, the details of the past become ever smaller and less easy to discern as we travel down the road of time.

Remembering what we call history poses a special challenge. First of all, if we have not experienced its events, they come to us secondhand and so lack personal immediacy. And if those events took place long ago, the characters who took part in them may look alien to us because they dress in clothes or speak in dialects very different from our own.

Most of all, history is hard to remember because there's so much of it, and the "so much" keeps growing every day. In fact, knowing history is much harder than it was centuries ago, simply because there are more centuries to recall!

Egypt's pharaohs, for example, never had to study Greek history, and the Classical Greeks never had to learn about the Renaissance. Chronological order spared them that obligation. Thus, King Tut did not have to read Plato, and Plato did not have to read Shakespeare. We, on the other hand, hold the dirty end of the chronological stick. Like a player in a perverse version of the game "I Pack My Trunk," whoever's turn is last must memorize the most.

The problem of recalling the past has thus been compounded by the multiple legacies we have inherited. As creatures of time, each of us is the end product of a sequence of cultural epochs that reach back thousands of years. Like the DNA that records our genetic past, our cultural matrix is inscribed with the values and experiences of earlier times.

We may ignore our ancestry if we wish, and elect to be cultural orphans. Or we may search out our parentage. If we choose to search, however, our mission will not be easy. Pushing through the crowded terminal of civilization, we will have to hang on not only to our own luggage but the bulging, clumsy trunks of previous ages. No wonder so many high school and college students, faced with such a daunting task, resort to hiring Cliff, the friendly porter, to help carry their bags.

But while *Cliffs Notes* may help a student pass an exam, they can't help a whole civilization pass the more challenging test of time. To do that, a people must have a deeper insight into themselves, one provoked by a reasoned confrontation with tradition, and such a confrontation suffers from abridgment.

Nor have the resources at our disposal made our job any easier. In fact, they've made it harder. In ancient times, poets and the elderly told and retold the same treasured stories, already ingrained in the hearts of those who heard them. New tales might be invented but their number was small.

As the centuries rolled on, however, more and more events took place, and a bigger and bigger inventory of facts piled up in the warehouse of history. The sheer bulk of it all has made it not only impossible to know everything but nearly impossible even to know what is worth knowing. The printed page, the flypaper of human thought, attracts and adheres to itself all the buzzing and expiring minutiae of existence. By making possible the mass production and collection of books, the printing press exponentially expanded the burden of what could be learned and made the task of comprehensive learning intimidating. To make matters worse, today's electronic storage and transmission of data daily drowns us in a recurring flood of new information.

For the ancients, who had less to remember, things were easier. Though about eight hundred years separated the Classical Greeks from the Trojan War, they remembered it clearly thanks to their bards who faithfully passed on the story by word of mouth from generation to generation until it was committed to writing. Even the Romans, whose Empire flourished five centuries later, preserved the Trojan War's memory until it was poetically enshrined in Vergil's *Aeneid*.

Roman history was still alive almost two thousand years later in the days of the English historian, Edward Gibbon. Gibbon could be described as one of the earliest pollsters in history. An eighteenth-century contemporary of Thomas Jefferson, Gibbon believed civilization had reached its apex in the days of ancient Rome. He then set about trying to figure out why Rome had fallen. His research was eventually summed up in grand style in a massive, multivolume work called *The Decline and Fall of the Roman Empire*, one of the true classics of Western literature.

In introducing the theme of his work, Gibbon made the following assertion:

> If a man were called to fix the period in the history of the world during which the condition of the human race was most happy and prosperous, he would, without hesitation, name that which elapsed from the death of Domitian to the accession of Commodus.[4]

Now let's imagine a contemporary pollster putting the same question to a typical group of Americans. How many of them would answer by naming the time of the Roman Empire as humanity's finest hour? More importantly, how many would even know what time the Roman Empire was? And how many could recognize the names of emperors like "Domitian" or "Commodus"? Or even know what "accession" means?

Now, for the purposes of our investigation, let's ignore the whole question of whether the ancient Romans really *were* the happiest or richest people in history. After all, a lot of different civilizations have come and gone since Gibbon's day. Instead, let's focus on two telling phrases in Gibbon's statement. He begins with these words: "If a man were called upon . . ." Leaving aside the sexist implications of the phrase (which in fact honestly reflect the biased realities of schooling in Gibbon's day), what our author is saying is this: "The answer I am about to provide is one any educated person of my day would be expected to give." To which Gibbon adds: "without hesitation." In short, to Gibbon the question was virtually rhetorical: had any educated person been asked it, Gibbon says, that person's reply would have been predictable and immediate.

It's easy to become depressed by Gibbon's high level of confidence in his fellow Englishmen, especially after we reflect on the modern surveys presented in this book. Such a comparison casts doubt on any simplistic notion of human progress. How could eighteenth-century Englishmen have known so much? How could we have remembered so little?

Of course, there's an easy explanation for why Gibbon's Englishmen appear so much more knowledgeable than do we. After all, they were closer to the Roman Empire chronologically. Therefore they remembered more about it than we do.

Now to some extent this argument has merit. But how much closer *were* they? Gibbon lived thirteen centuries after the fall of Rome—quite a long time by any standard. And we are only two centuries removed from his time. Are those two centuries enough to explain our relatively greater ignorance of ancient times?

And what about the Trojan War? Eight centuries separated the Classical Greeks from that encounter. Yet *they* remembered it. And to the Imperial Romans, the Trojan War was twelve centuries old. And yet they remembered it too.

In fact, as we've already seen in chapter 1, Americans—even American college students—are abysmally ignorant not only of events that took place centuries ago, but even of events that took place just a few years ago in our own country. If today even relatively recent history blurs in the memory, there must be some other factor or factors—other than the simple passage of time—that can explain such gross and progressive cultural amnesia.

The Urgent Call of the Senses

Our penchant to forget goes hand in hand with our capacity to remember. We let go of what we no longer need as though to make room on memory's shelf for what we currently require. And so, memories that are no longer useful are allowed—like old telephone numbers—to fade away.

But our attitude toward the past is also determined by the primitive need to survive. Out of biological necessity, primitive consciousness automatically assigned to the present a higher priority than it did to the past. Danger lurked in the here and now, and hunger and thirst cried out for immediate satisfaction. Thus the present had an instinctual primacy the past did not. So was it always in the life of Stone Age tribes as it was of lower animals. And so does it continue to be: to survive we must deal with now.

Pleasure also speaks through the lips of the present. The pleasure we experience in gratifying our senses exists in the now, not the then.

Thus the language of our nerve endings is a patois of the present. The intellect may conjure up images of what once was (the past) or what yet could be (the future), but appetite and its fulfillment belong to now.[5]

The Devaluation of the Past

The Value of Tradition. Despite the primacy of the present, the experiences of the past have nevertheless been vital to human beings from their beginnings as a race.

As a source of practical knowledge (how to make tools and weapons, how and where to find food and shelter), the past—like the present—aided survival. The collective wisdom of the tribe was therefore passed on as tradition from one generation to the next. To this was added the tales of the gods and the teachings of the priests, at first transmitted orally and then, with the birth of civilization, enshrined in sacred scripture. The past thus became a source of moral guidance and a stabilizing force as people journeyed through time to an unseen future. Ancient societies cultivated the art of memory as they reverently looked back to the past for precedent and direction.

When the Greeks struggled through periods of chaos and change, they turned for inspiration to their legendary heroes. From this mythic connectedness with the past, they drew courage to face adversity.

Likewise, the early Romans modeled their morals on the ways of their ancestors. The two-faced Roman god Janus—one face turned back to the past, the other ahead to the future—symbolized the Roman respect for the guiding power of tradition.

Following the fall of Rome, Christianity became a spiritual anchor for Europeans tossed on the turbulent sea of the Dark Ages. Even though the New Testament was centuries old, and the Old Testament centuries older, the stories of the Bible and the lessons they taught became for the Middle Ages a compass for the voyage of the human soul.

From the Renaissance to the Enlightenment of the eighteenth century, the Classical and Biblical traditions became the combined foundation for Western education and thought, and the joint stimuli for artistic and literary creativity. No wonder then that Thomas Jefferson and his colonial colleagues were thoroughly schooled in the philosophy and history of ancient times.[6] Rather than inhibiting them from thinking new thoughts, the heritage of the past energized the direction of their dreams for human freedom and social justice. Jefferson and his contemporaries were intimate with ancient history, not because they were amateur antiquarians, but because they were realists who clearly understood that "history is the only laboratory to test the consequence of human thought."[7] To them, the experiences of the ancient Greeks and Romans—their successful experiments with democracy and their tragic failures—offered moral insights into how to construct a free and just republic.[8]

The Power of Science and Technology. In the nineteenth century the rise of science and technology combined to devalue the past and undermine the importance of memory. Science challenged the validity of age-old tradition (including religious tradition), while technology demonstrated that the antiquated things of the past deserved to be replaced. As their successes mounted in the late nineteenth and twentieth centuries, forward-looking science and advanced technology more and more displaced the backward-looking humanities—focused on books already written and deeds already done—as subjects worthy of study and attention.[9] As for memory, the modern age would invent an agile surrogate for the human mind: the computer, a device in which memories (even the most personal) can be stored in disembodied form to be later accessed at will—that is, if we remember.

By creating the impression that the new is intrinsically superior to the old, science and technology effectively dethroned tradition. Simultaneously, they also elevated the stature of the present and future in the human mind.

The Acceleration of Change. For tens of thousands of years, most changes human beings experienced came from one of two places: their own bodies and the natural world that surrounded them. From their own bodies they knew need and gratification, pleasure and pain, effort and rest, wakefulness and sleep; from the natural world, daylight and darkness, heat and cold, and seasonal change.

As complex civilizations arose and spread, more and more changes began to come not from nature but from the artificial world human beings had created, a world fabricated by man. With population growth and the expansion of cities, the artificial world began to dominate an environment that previously had been exclusively natural.

This artificial world was markedly different from the natural one in the way it expressed and embodied change. While nature tended to regenerate and repeat itself in regular cycles, the artificial world was characterized by novelty and instability. Technology did not repeat itself but advanced, and did so with increasing momentum as each new innovation generated others. As human labor and the power of domesticated animals were augmented by mechanization, the tempo of civilization picked up. With the industrial and electronic revolutions, a mostly manmade world became feasible, a continually changing inorganic environment comprised of artifices, artifacts, and images of unending multiplicity, variety, and complexity, moving at greater and greater speed.[10]

We are surrounded by that environment today. The transformations it has undergone in just the last few decades are dramatic. The first personal computer, for example, appeared in 1970; by 1984, only eight out of one hundred households had one; by 1994, one out of three.[11] And every eighteen months for decades now, computer speed has doubled. Only one hundred thousand fax machines were sold in 1983; today, the number is over two million.[12] And today, some thirty million Americans carry electronic pagers, fifteen times the number that did just a decade ago.[13] Nor has the rate of change abated. On an almost daily basis, the *New York Times* and the *Wall Street Journal* report stunning new technical developments with far-reaching implications, especially in the allied fields of electronics, computers, and telecommunications. Indeed, at its current rate of growth, within another decade the electronics industry may in fact become the largest industry in the world, second only to the production of food.

Rapid change has in fact become the most dominant characteristic of the society in which we live. Indeed, it is so prevalent a force that its presence is often taken as normal. Though change has always been a fact of life, the *rate* of change today makes it a psychological and social phenomenon unique in human history.

What is more, technological developments do not simply affect the way business operates or the kinds of devices we use in our everyday lives. They also design and construct an invisible high-speed environment within our minds, one in which the past and the memory of the past have little place.

Never before in history have the minds of so many people been simultaneously immersed in the swirling waters of transience and impermanence. And of all countries this is most true of America, where the blessings of technology are so evident. The essence of these rushing waters has soaked into our consciousness and our souls. It has become the very blood that now surges with increasing velocity through our veins.

Change, without doubt, can be salutary. It has always been the most compelling reason to go on a vacation—to "get away from it all" and experience new and different things. On a distant beach or on a cruise ship we can forget about familiar responsibilities because we are far removed from all the associations that remind us of work. Remembering, after all, relies on such connections, and anything that can dissolve them allows us to forget and relax—at least until our return flight touches down and we go back home.

Even in our daily routine, change can be stimulating and invigorating. And who can deny the value of changes wrought by science and technology that have made our lives easier, safer, and healthier—or those wrought by political means that have made our lives more free?

All of this is true. But there is also a downside. An excess of change, especially if it is persistent and urgent, can induce stress.[14] By compelling us to adjust and readjust to new circumstances and demands, change can destabilize our existence. When things move too fast, we lose perspective on our priorities as we frantically strive just to keep up. Should an entire society exhibit such behavior, its symptoms may come to resemble those of a nervous breakdown, but on a massive social scale. More then twenty-five years ago, Alvin Toffler recognized the signs in America. He termed the condition "future shock," a condition caused by "too much change in too short a time."[15] "[U]nless man quickly learns to control the rate of change . . . ," Toffler said, "we are doomed to a massive adaptational breakdown."[16]

Rapid change, however, can produce other social effects, more subtle than future shock but even more devastating to the long-term future of civilization. By overwhelming us with new stimuli, rapid change takes our attention off the past. Indeed, why remember anything when it will be gone so soon? Whether the stimuli are painful or pleasurable does not matter: the end result is the same—the past is displaced by an insistent present.

Of course, who would expect anything else? In an urgent situation, we rarely have time to look back. Instead, we have to deal with the problems at hand.

Nevertheless, the question of *how* we deal with those problems will still remain. Will we deal with them effectively as individuals if in our hurry we forget who we are, if we lose sight of the things we have always stood for and believed in? And will we deal with them effectively as a people if in our haste we forget who we are as a nation, if we lose sight of what history has recorded and what our collective goals have always been?

Nor are we simply dealing with an isolated emergency. The rush of events in our society has increased to such a degree, and the pressures of everyday existence risen so much, that urgency has become commonplace.

It is said that Abraham Lincoln had time to open his own mail, and President McKinley time to answer his own phone.[17] America's current president certainly has no such luxury. But leisure has become a luxury in the minds of a growing number of average citizens as well. When asked in 1965 if their lives felt rushed all the time, 25 percent of those surveyed said yes.[18] By 1975, the figure was 28 percent.[19] By 1985, 32 percent.[20] By 1992, 38 percent, and not just "rushed," but "rushed all the time."[21] In fact, those surveyed felt pressured even when they were trying to relax.[22]

As a result of modern scientific and technological advances, we increasingly live in a society of speed, a speed engendered and sustained by electronic technologies that operate at the velocity of light. More and more, society's structure comes to resemble an electronic circuit in which being "on line" is akin to life itself. In such a society, permanence and constancy are replaced by transience and flux. We "go with the flow," transported on a commercialized stream of pulsating sensory stimulation. We are "screenies," creatures of the screen—the movie screen, the television screen, the computer screen—mesmerized by momentary dots glistening on cold glass. We live in a hyperculture, ruled by the power of now, the tyranny of an all-exclusive present uncompromised by any other realm of time.[23] Nothing lasts for us, but it no longer matters, not as long as new moments continue to come. And as our consciousness fuses with the media around us, *they* become our memory, a memory that continually changes.

Under the pressured influence of high-speed living, the structure of the family has broken down,[24] leaving us without humanity's prime transmitter of tradition. If mothers and fathers are no longer able to read their children stories, if they no longer have time to tell them remembered tales, who will the storytellers be, and what tales will be told?

No wonder the past has receded from our thoughts. We have little time for it since our lives move so fast. Besides it is so hard to see. Like the scenery rushing by the window of a speeding car, the past becomes a blur.

The Lure of Materialism

The mood of transience created by technology has been reinforced by America's economic success.

By helping to make more goods and services available to more people, advances in technology have raised the level of our wealth and comfort. As a result, material possessions have become a more prevalent aspect of our everyday life. But their availability and appeal has also fostered materialism as a way of life. More and more, our identities are defined by our role as consumers.[25]

In a consumer society, companies can multiply their profits by making and selling goods that are frequently replaced because they no longer work or are no longer desired. Thus companies grow rich by planned obsolescence and the manipulation of desire.

By appealing to our desire, materialism elevates the senses as the determinant of our choices. The greater the focus on the senses and sensory gratification, as we have seen, the greater the emphasis on the present as the prime source of meaning in life. As a consequence, the affluence and economic structure of our society combine to create a psychological environment in which what is old—including the past—is regarded as useless and obsolete.

Meanwhile, a pervasive entertainment industry prevents boredom by profitably presenting an ever shifting array of new stimulations and intellectual diversions. At the same time, a drug industry—legal and illegal—thrives by selling consumers the means to keep up with the speed of society, slow down to escape its unnatural pace, or enjoy intense pleasures that ordinary society seems unable to provide.

The Newness of Our Nation

America is especially susceptible to the devaluation of memory because its own history is so short. Unlike Europeans or Asians, Americans lack deep historical roots because their country came into existence only a little more than two centuries ago. We are a nation of newcomers in a New World, a revolutionary nation committed not to the past but to progress and the future.[26]

Most of all, as Americans we believe in "the pursuit of happiness," and that means pursuing the new things that will give us happiness. We care little about history because we have little history to care about. Instead, it is now that matters.

To the extent that America has been fertile ground for the growth of the Industrial and Electronic revolutions, whatever roots memory might have put down have gone into shallow soil. Because both revolutions have been predicated on rapid change, they have made Americans strangers to tradition, and a culture alien to tradition is a culture hostile to memory. Even the physical landscape of our country changes before our eyes as old buildings are torn down to make way for new ones and natural tracts are bulldozed to make way for subdivisions.

Democracy itself contributes to the decline of memory. By responding to the current wishes of its citizens, democracy offers its allegiance to the present. By advocating equality, it not only reduces distinctions between social groups but also diminishes the value of their separate histories. In its melting pot for over a century, ethnic memories have been readily exchanged for the benefits of citizenship. And while the multiculturalist movement of today seeks to recapture such memories, it often furthers its ends by rejecting that common history without which no nation can maintain its integrity.[27]

Despite our material success as a nation, many have come to feel that something is wrong, that something is missing, something lost, some part of us unanswered no matter what we get and spend or how quick we do it. "It's not enough," a voice in us says, "just to keep on going." Especially if our very speed makes us lose touch with who we are.

SCHOOLS AND SOCIETY

The social forces that induce us to forget are formidable. Paradoxically, their influence is transmitted through our schools, institutions whose purpose is to teach. Yet that is precisely where the problem lies. Our schools *do* teach.

A society's educational system, after all, is a reflection of its values and priorities. It follows, then, that the same forces that shape America's consciousness should also shape its schools. This fundamental principle must be recognized at the outset of our discussion. Otherwise, we might conclude that cultural amnesia can be cured by a curricular adjustment here or a pedagogical one there.

Yet nothing could be farther from the truth, for American public education will not be transformed until the American public is transformed. Anything short of this will yield results that are only marginal and temporary. Barring such an event, it is unlikely that changes will occur in schools substantive and deep enough to alter our national trajectory. That is because the course we are on is the one most Americans want to travel, conditioned as we are by the power of materialism and technology and the underlying premises of our nation.

It is now time to examine how America's schools and students have conformed to those forces.

The Role of Materialism

Amnesia in Ann Arbor. Richard Craig teaches communications at the University of Michigan, one of America's most selective and prestigious institutions of higher learning. According to Professor Craig, the students in his public opinion class are "bright, inquisitive, talented, and motivated."[28]

Yet these same students—mostly juniors and seniors—know very little about their country's history or government. When quizzed, only 7 percent were able to name Michigan's two U.S. senators, and scarcely a third could name America's secretary of state. Fewer than five out of ten knew when World War II had started or ended.[29]

Professor Craig was not surprised. Like you and me, he had read the results of national surveys of civic ignorance. What shocked him, however, was his students' attitude toward their ignorance. Rather than feel embarrassed or be surprised by how little they knew, they really didn't seem to care. "One student acted slightly offended that she should be expected to know these things," Craig reports. "'I know what I need to know,' she said. 'When is any of this stuff going to matter in my career?'"[30]

As Craig observes:

> After I assured her that being ignorant never helps, it occurred to me that she may have had a point. Many of my students have already planned highly specialized careers before they enter my class. More than a few have come to me explaining they would need to miss a lecture to interview with some corporation. These students are prized recruits, yet their future careers seldom require general historical knowledge. . . . These days students in their early teens are being told by their teachers and parents to start working on a career plan right away, and from that point forward they choose their courses of study to fit that plan. Children discover quickly that specialized knowledge within their chosen field is what's really important. Knowing why there was a cold war just doesn't matter.[31]

"Will It Get Me a Job?" The attitudes expressed by Professor Craig's class are shared by large numbers of high school and college students across the country.

A 1996 survey of high school students conducted by Public Agenda, a Washington, DC-based nonprofit research group,[32] found that fewer than half of the students polled felt it was important to study American history or geography. Moreover, only 18 percent thought it important to read the works of modern American writers. Instead, most emphasized the importance of practical job skills (59 percent), especially computer skills (75 percent).

Certainly, young people like these shouldn't be condemned for wanting marketable skills. What is lamentable is the way they demean subjects that can't be converted into cash.

It's easy, though, to understand where their attitudes come from. Growing up in a society where money has become the universal standard for

measuring worth, including one's own, they have become young materialists. Teenagers, in fact, are already one of the most potent consumer groups,
spending about $100 billion in the marketplace every year.[33]

The School as Marketplace. If we believe, however, that there are some
things that money can't buy, that not everything—including some of the
most precious things in life—can or should be measured in money, then
surely that is a message we must communicate to our children by word and
deed, at home and elsewhere.

If the young are exposed to rampant commercialism in the outside world,
certainly the school ought to be one zone that is commercial-free. Unfortu-
nately, that is no longer the case. More and more, the classroom is becoming
the place where children see and hear commercials.

Corporations have been quick to capitalize on the captive audience in our
country's schools by distributing "free" materials to teachers and principals.[34] "Learning" kits, complete with posters, videos, and activity sheets
convey information on subjects like ecology, economics, social studies,
money management, health, safety, and food—all with a capitalistic corporate slant. At the same time, brand-name products are celebrated through
corporate-sponsored school contests and incentive programs.

It's a typical school day in America. 7:00 a.m. America's School Kid
rolls out of bed, rubs her eyes, and gets ready for school. After grab-
bing a bite, she's ready to go. But while she's walking out the door, she
remembers that she left her algebra book on the table. She runs back
and grabs it, remembering it's the one with the bright Nike cover that
her school issued her.

8:00 a.m. A yellow school bus picks up America's School Kid at
the corner. Its top and sides are painted with large signs advertising
7–Up.

8:30 a.m. The yellow bus pulls up to school, and America's School
Kid rushes through its doors, makes her way past a bulletin board
beckoning her to visit Jan's Beauty Shop, and ducks into the home
room class where her teacher is writing today's announcements on a
class calendar sporting an insurance-company logo.

As our kid settles down to do her homework, today's 12–minute,
ad-financed Channel One news broadcast for students begins to air.
Four minutes into the program she looks up to see a hip-looking teen-
ager downing a Pepsi on screen—in the same ad currently being
shown on MTV.[35]

Broadcast by satellite Monday through Friday to as many as twelve thousand schools, Channel One reaches some seven million students from grades six to twelve, over 40 percent of America's teenage population.[36] Programs intermix twelve minutes of current events with two minutes of commercials (Opening credits / News: Teamsters strike, labor relations / Ad for Mountain Dew / Ad for Crest toothpaste / Part 4: Drinking and driving / Feature: Pop quiz (What Teamsters' President disappeared?) / Anti-drug ad / Ad for Noxema / Answer to Pop quiz (Jimmy Hoffa) / End).[37]

The Faustian bargain school boards make is that they get free video recorders plus a nineteen-inch television set for every classroom. All they have to do is show Channel One on nine out of ten school days in 80 percent of their classrooms. For most equipment-poor schools, the inducement is too much to pass up.[38] But, as a result, the classroom comes to reinforce the materialistic values current in society at large.

And when students leave high school, those that go on to college carry their materialistic attitudes with them.

Philosophy vs. Cash. Since 1968, the American Council on Education in cooperation with the University of California at Los Angeles Education Research Institute has been sampling freshman attitudes at two- and four-year colleges and universities. In the fall of 1997, for example, they queried more than a quarter of a million such students at almost five hundred institutions.[39] When the freshmen were asked what objectives they considered essential or very important, 74.9 percent listed "being very well off financially." But only 40.8 percent thought highly of "developing a meaningful philosophy of life."[40]

Strikingly, these figures were an almost exact reverse of what the poll had shown in 1968.[41] Then, 82.5 percent had viewed developing a meaningful philosophy of life as an essential or very important goal, while only 40.8 percent had favored financial well-being. Over the course of some thirty years—from the late 1960s to the late 1990s—the appeal of materialism had gradually grown on campus while the appeal of nonmaterial values had declined.

According to Linda J. Sax, director of the 1997 study, students were looking at education more as a means than an end instead of valuing what was learned for its own sake.[42] The results of the survey tended to confirm the impressions of college teachers and administrators that students "view higher education less as an opportunity to expand their minds and more as a means to increase their incomes."[43] In the words of Mark W. Edmundson, who teaches English at the University of Virginia, "Schooling has become more about training and less about transformation."[44]

One of the most depressing aspects of these findings is an apparent decline of idealism among the young. As far back as the days of Aristotle, idealism had been identified as one of youth's most distinguishing traits.[45] That is because the expansive hopefulness of youth has not yet been exposed to the persistent abrasion of disappointment that produces the narrower realism or cynicism of later age. But when such idealism is missing even among the young, what hope can remain for society at large?

Surely students should not be faulted for realistically appraising the job market they will encounter when they leave the ivy-covered walls of their college. But if a desire for affluence becomes the main reason for choosing their majors, students will be cheating themselves, especially if they also pick the easiest, rather than the most personally challenging, electives.

College may be about making a living; but it must also be about making a life. Indeed, discovering who you are may be the best way to discover what to become. Sadly, many students who do pick the path of enlightenment come home on holidays to find themselves badgered by anxious parents who ask: "What good will studying *that* do you?"

A Means to an End. Under the influence of materialism, job-smart students apply to universities not because of a school's true commitment to undergraduate education[46] but because of the school's "prestige" which can later be parlayed into lucrative employment offers and salaries. Under materialism's spell, college becomes, in the words of the late Ernest R. Boyer, a mere "credentialing exercise. It's not seen as a serious intellectual quest. . . . The aim is to figure out what you need to get through this system.[47] As a result, many students play the angles. As educated consumers, they appeal grades that might impede their financial goals and, in increasing numbers, resort to cheating to insure the highest grades with the least expenditure of effort.[48]

Of course, if there was no monetary pay-off for a degree, most campuses would be radically depopulated. But society has made having a diploma a job requirement, even when the course of study is not related to the job. As a result, graduating from a university has become a kind of intelligence test run for the convenience of corporate human resource departments.

The Corruption of the Liberal Arts. Meanwhile, back on the mega-campus, professors are busily engaged in research to advance their own careers, leaving the actual task of instruction to overworked and underpaid assistants.[49] Up in the tower, administrators huddle, devising marketing strategies to please the pragmatic board of governors, largely comprised of businessmen. They formulate market-driven plans, typically rewarding programs that attract the most students or research grants, and penalizing those programs that don't with attrition or extinction by denying them replacements when their faculty retire or die. More and more they allow the complexion of the university to mirror society's own commercial face rather than challenging society's conceit and their own by holding their blemishes up to the critical standard of another era.

In such an educational system the humanities will have little place. Materialism, after all, is concerned with the tangible; the humanities, with the intangible. Materialism deals in the temporary; the humanities, in what is timeless.

No wonder the two are so hopelessly at odds; no wonder neither side comprehend the other's logic.[50] In the end, the liberal arts can never make concessions to materialism, unless they are corrupted, because their defining virtue is to liberate, or free, us so we can reach toward higher things.[51]

The stuff of memory, like the humanities themselves, is equally intangible. Memories are priceless and cannot be bought or sold. Moreover, they endure in a way that superficial sensation does not. Because of these likenesses to the humanities, memory and the study of history are also belittled by materialists, except as tools to demonstrate how much better off we are today than yesterday. In an educational institution dominated by materialism, the study of the collective memory of our race will always be subordinated to other, crasser needs.

The Role of Technology

Today, technology plays a greater role in humanity's everyday life than ever before in history. Mechanical and, more recently, electronic devices have replaced human labor and made our lives more effortless. As a result, the quality of our existence has come to be defined by the technology that surrounds us.

The Technological Assumption. One of the psychological consequences is the "technological assumption," an attitude conditioned by the multiplicity of times technology is used each day. Habituated to the use of non-human means to accomplish its purposes, a society comes to assume that when a task needs doing—even an educational task—technology is the answer.

But what if there is a category of problems for which a technological solution is inappropriate? The tendency to apply technology may persist none the less. In such a case, a technological fix will at best create the illusion of having effectively addressed the problem. At worst, it may actually deepen the problem by deceiving us into thinking we are making progress when in fact we are not. In a society pervaded by technology, technology becomes the recourse of the first, second, and even third resort to improve life even when it is unsuited to the task. In a society pervaded by materialism, money is regarded the same way. And when a society is both technological *and* materialistic, the more expensive a technology is, the more valuable and useful it is imagined to be. Should its price go down, it becomes a "bargain."

Even as technology changes the outer world we live in, it also changes the inner one of our consciousness. Our values and priorities tend to be those that match the mechanical and electronic universe we inhabit. We become, in Thoreau's words, "the tools of our tools."[52] As a result, the exhilaration of technological speed and its efficacy lead people to value speed more than ever before, diminishing in their eyes the worth of activities that take time, including the time-consuming activity of learning.

Speed and Memory. If remembering takes time and memorizing still more, such activities are assigned to technological surrogates: the electric calculator, the spell-checking word processor, the personal computer. As a corollary, parallel powers atrophy in the human mind: the clerk cannot add, the writer cannot spell, the busy executive cannot remember.

Remembrance, however, is a distinctively human activity whose transformative function cannot be accomplished by the warehousing of data in an electronic alter ego. If memories are not a living part of us, they cannot enrich our inner lives or inform our vocations.[53]

When we studied personal memory in chapter 2, we learned that the persistence of memory depends upon the integration of new information with old, that we remember things best in the environment where we first learned them, and that emotional experiences can leave the most lasting impressions on our minds. A high-speed culture, however, conspires to erode the very foundations of memory.

First of all, it hurls more stimuli at us than we can possibly comprehend or absorb, leaving us little time or opportunity to integrate what we have just learned with the things we already knew. Secondly, since the framework of our existence is in constant and rapid flux and the world is literally changing before our eyes, we no longer have a reliable hook on which to hang our memories. Thirdly, through overstimulation the pulsating hyperculture we inhabit induces a type of stress that chemically interferes with the very process of remembering. Our amnesia is not caused by a single physical trauma but rather by a sustained cultural electroshock that numbs our power of retention. Short-term memories slip down a greased slope to oblivion that long-term historical memories have no chance to even climb.

Speed and Creativity. Technological speed also depreciates the value of creative and psychologically restorative activities that are inherently slow and time-intensive: contemplation, reflection, meditation, appreciation. All these activities that provide perspective are just so much "down time" in a computer-driven world.

Nonquantitative activities of the human spirit are demeaned because they do not conform to physical laws and often challenge society's own dehumanizing premises. Thus technology inevitably narrows the range of subjects taught at school. Grants may be given to improve training in mathematics and science, but much less so in the humanities, especially when the humanities focus on the past. Indeed, when students seek self-understanding, they are far more likely to turn to newer disciplines like sociology and psychology than to older ones like literature, philosophy, and history, whose roots in fact go farther back into time.

A Faded Motto. Like so many colleges and universities, the one where I teach has a motto: "Bonitatem et disciplinam et scientiam doce me." It means "Teach me goodness and judgment and knowledge."

The motto is in Latin, the language of the Catholic Church and, before that, of the Roman Empire. But the motto's sentiments are much older still. The words come from the Old Testament, a verse from an ancient Hebrew song (Psalm 119:66) in which the worshipper prays to God to instruct him in the ways of righteousness. The words of the motto are in Latin because they are taken from a translation made by St. Jerome around A.D. 400. Since my university was originally founded by Catholic priests, it is the Latin version they chose.

The motto embodies a set of priorities. The first and most important thing the psalmist prays to be taught is "bonitas" (goodness), then "disciplina" (judgment), and lastly "scientia" (factual knowledge).[54] The spiritual basis for this gradation is clear: facts alone are inadequate unless we possess a capacity for critical judgment; yet even that capacity is inadequate if not infused with goodness. Thus, of all subjects the most important is moral.

Over the more than thirty years I have been a professor at my university, I have seen changes in its curriculum that parallel similar changes in society.

It is "scientia" (factual knowledge) that has risen and "bonitas" (goodness) that has sunk as a subject worthy of study. As courses in the natural and social sciences have multiplied, programs in religion, philosophy, and the Classics have declined, often not because of a lack of genuine student interest as much as because of administrative bias.

To be fair, the administrators are right. They, better than I, know what is popular. And their judgment is confirmed by graphs reflecting enrollment patterns for the last three decades in colleges and universities across America.[55]

Each year I quiz my classes to see if they recognize "Bonitatem et disciplinam et scientiam." A couple of hands may go up in a class of a hundred. These are the students who recognize their school's motto. If I then ask the class what the words mean, not a single hand is raised.

Such a survey reflects not just the decline of Latin or of Biblical literacy, but something much deeper: the forgetting of both words and their symbolic meaning. By losing touch with a motto, my students have lost touch with an outlook on life.

It may well be argued that the world no longer needs spiritual guidance, that secular values are sufficient to take us into—and beyond—the twenty-first century. But what offends me is that my students are not granted the power to choose. Materialism and technology have effectively revised the curriculum, foreclosing not only whole subjects but an entire set of human alternatives once known but now deliberately hurled down an Orwellian memory chute.[56] Aldous Huxley foresaw this academic outcome in *Brave New World*.

He waved his hand; and it was as though, with an invisible feather whisk, he had brushed away a little dust, and the dust was Harappa, was Ur of the Chaldees; some spider-webs, and they were Thebes and Babylon and Cnossos and Mycenae. Whisk. Whisk—and where was Odysseus, where was Job, where were Jupiter and Gotama and Jesus? Whisk—and those specks of antique dirt called Athens and Rome, Jerusalem and the Middle Kingdom—all were gone. Whisk—the place where Italy had been was empty. Whisk, the cathedrals; whisk, whisk, King Lear and the Thoughts of Pascal. Whisk, Passion; whisk, Requiem; whisk, Symphony; whisk. . . .[57]

Technology has done the whisking by pointing us toward some subjects and away from others.

Two particular technologies merit our attention. Together they are having as much influence on learning today as the printing press had in earlier times. In fact if they have their way, they may just undo the printing press itself. These two technologies are television and the computer. Like electroshock therapy applied with low voltages every day, they are subtly erasing our sense of a past.

Television: Selling the Present. The electronic innovation that has had the most impact on America's memory is television.

Though TV sets can be found in schools, television's greatest influence occurs at home. According to *TV Guide*, the average American spends ten years of his or her life watching television, and two whole years just watching commercials.[58]

Because television's audience is so big, advertisers in 1996 spent more money buying commercial time—$36 billion—than the federal government spent on education. In prime time, you'll see an average of thirty-seven nonprogram messages every hour, and fifty of them in daytime. All these commercials are being broadcast for one purpose: to "educate" you. Television, in fact, is the one school we go to all our lives. It's the one school we never graduate from, and therefore the one that teaches us the most.[59]

If that's the case, what do we learn from our electric *alma mater*? And how does television affect our memory?

To begin with, every viewer majors in materialism. That's the one message all the commercials have in common: you're nothing unless you buy. What you bought yesterday doesn't matter; you've got to buy today.

As we've already seen, the emphasis of materialism is on immediate gratification. The present is what counts—not the past. The only time a commercial will use the past is if the ad agency thinks nostalgia will help sell the product. Memory will then be used, but not cherished for its own sake. There are exceptions—the popularity of A & E's "Biography" series and the promise of the History Channel[60]—but these are exceptions. As a medium of instancy, television prefers the now of news to the then of history.

Fragmenting Time. Commercials have another effect: by their presence they undermine a show's continuity. Of course, we don't notice the effect much, but that's the point. Commercials accustom us to *dis*continuity.

So what does this have to do with our memory of the past, you ask. Everything. Memory requires connectedness because history is a whole in which past, present, and future are joined. Anything that snaps that lifeline will set us adrift in time.

Children are especially vulnerable to television's influence because their minds are still forming. By training children to be passive viewers, television prepares them to become impassive pupils. By entertaining them, it leads them to expect the same in school. Disappointed when teachers don't "perform" or assignments "amuse," they soon grow restive and bored.

Stunting Brains. In her book, *Endangered Minds*,[61] Jane Healy persuasively argued that children who watch too much television fail to develop the neural circuitry they will eventually need to understand complex sentences and ideas. Denied the stimulus of physical activity, conversation, and reading, their brains acquire a different wiring, one that will later handicap their ability to concentrate and analyze. Healy presents biological evidence to suggest that such wiring may be irreversible.

As America's TV-watching kids move on to high school and even college, publishers dumb down their books—simplifying sentences, eliminating "difficult" words, and adding colorful pictures to give students the illusion of success and to make the lives of teachers easier.[62]

In one respect, however, television *can* contribute to literacy. As the cartoon father reprimanded his cartoon son: "If you don't learn to read, you'll never be able to find out what's going to be on television."[63]

Cyberdreams and Reality. Like television, the computer is now playing a major role in shaping attitudes toward learning outside and inside school.

A computer's novelty sets it apart from such older tools of learning as books. To a culture enamored of technology, the computer has immediate appeal. Its typewriter keyboard doesn't even sound like an old-fashioned typewriter. And its screen shows us the face of a friend, television, but a friend that is so much more responsive to our individual needs than our old friend television ever was. It gives us what we want instantly (or almost instantly). It can make us smart, and it can make us money, because if we're computer literate—we're told—we can get a job.

For principals and school boards, for academic vice-presidents and boards of governors, it's been love at first sight. What could be better than a teacher you don't have to negotiate with every year, a teacher that can be periodically upgraded and won't ever complain? What could be better than "an America where every child can stretch a hand across a keyboard and reach every book ever written, every painting ever painted, every symphony ever composed."[64]

The possibilities are limitless, but so are the questions. First of all, where is the estimated $50 billion coming from to buy the computers, wire the schools, and train the teachers to meet Bill Clinton's goal of connecting every school in the country to the Internet by the year 2000.[65] And even if the money could someday be found, should this be the way we spend it?

As critic Clifford Stoll maintains: "Computers solve a problem that doesn't exist. The one thing they do well is bring more information into the classroom. But I've never heard teachers complain about a lack of information. The real problems . . . are class size, shrinking attention spans, a lack of discipline, and drugs and guns."[66] As one ninth-grade English teacher complains: "As a learning tool I think they're overrated. We've spent so much in our library on computers and comparatively little on books."[67]

Indeed, independent research has yet to demonstrate a clear and convincing connection between student achievement and computer use. According to Edward Miller, a former editor of *Harvard Education Letter*: "Most knowledgeable people agree that most of the research isn't valid. It's so flawed it shouldn't even be called research. Essentially, it's just worthless."[68] Esther Dyson, a member of the Clinton Administration's task force on technology, agrees. Says Dyson: "In this area there is little proof."[69] The issue is best summarized by Jane Healy in her book, *Failure to Connect*:

Today's children are the subjects of a vast and optimistic experiment. It is well financed and enthusiastically supported by major corporations, the public at large, and government officials around the world. If it is successful, our youngsters' minds and lives will be enriched, society will benefit, and education will be permanently changed for the better. But there is no proof—or even convincing evidence—that it will work. . . .

While some very exciting and potentially valuable things are happening between children and computers, we are currently spending far too much money with too little thought. It is past time to pause, reflect, and ask some probing questions.[70]

Adds critic Todd Oppenheimer:

The solution is not to ban computers from classrooms altogether. But it may be to ban federal spending on what is fast becoming an overheated campaign.

If schools can impose some limits—on technology donors and on themselves—rather than indulging in a consumer frenzy, most will probably find themselves with more electronic gear than they need. That could free the billions Clinton wants to devote to technology and make it available for impoverished fundamentals: teaching solid skills in reading, thinking, listening, and talking; organizing inventive field-trips and other rich hands-on experiences; and, of course, building up the nation's core of knowledgeable, inspiring teachers. These notions are considerably less glamorous than computers are, but their worth is firmly proved through a long history.[71]

Yet, as long as it persists, the current emphasis on computers will continue to have a negative impact on our sense of a past.

To put it simply, all the books ever written aren't on-line, nor will they ever be. It would be prohibitively expensive to digitize them—$100 a book, according to one estimate, before taking into account the cost of copyright fees and necessary proofreading.[72]

While the computer gives the impression that it is a portal to all human knowledge, it is a door only to that knowledge that is electronically accessible. Tens of millions of books, especially older works, will never be scanned and will therefore remain invisible to those readers who only look at screens.

Because computers are mostly adept at serving up the new, they will serve up the present at the expense of the past. In turn, the popularity of computer literacy will paradoxically disinherit the public from literature's wealth. Indeed, classic works are already disappearing from library shelves, either de-selected by librarians because patrons no longer use them or disposed of as worn because replacing them would take away money already budgeted for monitors, CD-ROMs, and on-line services.[73] As the books are thrown out, so is our memory.

Computers can give us information, including access to documents and artifacts from the past.[74] What they cannot give us is a reason to value that past. They can give us more facts than we can ever use. What they cannot give us is judgment or goodness.[75]

As Neil Postman has cogently observed:

The computer argues . . . that the most serious problems confronting us at both personal and public levels require technical solutions through fast access to information otherwise unavailable. I would argue that this is, on the face of it, nonsense. Our most serious problems are not technical, nor do they arise from inadequate information. Where people are dying of starvation, it does not occur because of inadequate information. If families break up, children are mistreated, crime terrorizes a city, education is impotent, it does not happen because of inadequate information. Mathematical equations, instantaneous communication, and vast quantities of information have nothing whatever to do with any of these problems. And the computer is useless in addressing them.[76]

Such problems can only be solved if we are empowered by what Theodore Roszak has called "master ideas,"[77] "the great moral, religious, and metaphysical teachings which are the foundations of culture."[78] Yet as Roszak points out, "Master ideas are based on no information whatsoever."[79]

Regrettably, these ideas and, most important, our commitment to them, have so far been unable to solve all the problems of the world. An addiction to computers, however, can only make the problems worse, for our salvation belongs to a dimension no wires can ever reach.

The Role of History and National Beliefs

The nineteenth-century historian, Lord Acton, is famous for having said: "Power tends to corrupt and absolute power corrupts absolutely."[80] But another less well known maxim of his is worth noting: "All governments in which one principle dominates, degenerate by its exaggeration."[81]

We have already seen how the forces of materialism and technology have contributed to America's current state of amnesia. But cultural amnesia has another contributing cause, one that is rooted ironically in history itself and in a historic set of beliefs.

Dangerous Ideals. Some of the current trends in American education can be traced directly to the fundamental beliefs on which our nation was founded. It is from these principles that we derive our strength as a nation. But these same principles, carried to excess, now threaten our intellectual survival.

Americans have always been a nation of doers rather than a nation of thinkers, a race of makers rather than philosophers. This pragmatic streak in American character was evident over a century and a half ago to that famous

French tourist, Alexis de Tocqueville.[82] But the best proof of it is America's success in creating a culture of material plenty and technological power.

If we have philosophers, they were makers and doers as well, for they were the Founding Fathers who helped create our nation: Thomas Jefferson, James Madison, John Adams. The ideals they held high are enunciated in the Declaration of Independence, the Constitution, and the Bill of Rights: the ideals of freedom and equality. "We hold these Truths to be self-evident," wrote Jefferson, "that all Men are created equal, that they are endowed by their Creator with certain unalienable rights, that among these are Life, Liberty, and the Pursuit of Happiness."[83]

If we follow Lord Acton, however, we may be led to ask if our nation could perish by an exaggeration of these noble principles. Carry pragmatism too far, for example, and the academic result can be a three-R's back-to-the-basics movement in which "frills" like the humanities are dropped to make more room for instruction in marketable skills.

Take freedom and carry it to pedagogical excess and you get "anything goes."

> "We don't want to limit your freedom, Jill, so spell the words any way you want. Rules will only inhibit you and keep you from being creative."
>
> "Memorizing tables and equations, Jack, will only bore you. It's so hard and takes so much time. Why not have fun and guess at the answers instead?"

Over in ed school, the experts speak highly of "invented spelling,"[84] "the growth model of teaching composition,"[85] and "whole math,"[86] but meanwhile Jack and Jill tumble down the intellectual hill.

Take the pursuit of happiness to excess and you get the self-esteem movement[87] and grade inflation.[88] Add an excess of equality and you get no grades at all.[89]

From 1987 to 1997, combined SAT scores in the country fell fourteen points, but during the very same period high school averages of A increased 9 percent.[90] In Spokane, Washington, Ferris High School's Class of '97 had sixteen valedictorians, each with a perfect 4.0 grade-point average.[91] But the school board in Clark County, Nevada, had an even better idea. According to their plan

> [S]tudents who earn D's or below will be characterized not as border-line passing or failing but as *emerging*. Those earning A's will no

longer be commended for excellent work but will be told merely that they are *extending*, and those in between will not be described as doing adequate or mediocre work but [that] they are *developing*.[92]

That way nobody will be unhappy, and everybody's self-esteem will be protected. Thus in Spokane, academic life would imitate the mythical Lake Woebegone, where everyone's child is above average.[93]

To be sure, grade inflation masks real failure and creates only an illusion of success. To be sure also, there is little evidence—even after sixty-five hundred studies and thirty thousand articles—that self-esteem leads to academic achievement.[94] But bad ideas die hard, especially if they appeal to our basic instincts as a people.

Anti-intellectualism has had an especially powerful effect, especially in a technological society that tries to avoid effort as often as possible. A 1992 high school survey[95] revealed that only 41 percent of the school day was being spent on academic subjects. Filling the remaining 59 percent were practical classes in personal health and safety, consumer affairs, ecology, family life, and driver's ed, leaving only three hours a day for core courses in math, science, and history. After four years, American high school students had spent 1,460 hours studying these subjects. By comparison, Japanese students had spent 3,170; French students, 3,280; and German students, 3,528.[96] Thus American high schools spent less than half the class-time studying these subjects as did their Oriental and European counterparts. In fact, three-quarters of American high school seniors did less than five hours of homework a week.[97] For most American students, high school has been easy street.

And that's the way students want it. Over a three-year period, with the help of his colleagues, Professor Laurence Steinberg of Temple University surveyed twenty thousand public school students to get a picture of their lives and values.[98] "Academic achievement was so little valued that when asked which crowd they would like to be part of, many more students chose the "druggies" (one in six) than the "brains" (one in ten). The brains didn't think much of their position, either; half wished they were in a different crowd."[99]

The Challenge of Diversity. Our nation's history has also had an effect on what Americans learn. By definition, America is a country of immigrants. In its melting pot, those immigrants gave up their former citizenship for a piece of the American dream and were proud of the exchange they had made. Forgetting part of the past was the price of being "born on the Fourth of July."[100]

After more than a century, however, the pendulum has swung. In the words of Robert Hughes,[101] America has become a "culture of complaint," in which separate ethnic and racial groups view themselves as victims of discrimination whose achievements have never received credit. They challenge "e pluribus unum" by asserting that America is more "many" than it is "one," and reject the standard version of U.S. history that emphasizes the contributions of Protestant European whites.[102]

Multiculturalism, as the movement is called, can, in fact, be a misnomer. For, carried to excess, it can become not an assertion of America's diversity as much as a claim for special privilege—an argument for the part rather than for the whole. Preserving and celebrating one's heritage is the proud right of all Americans, but taken to an extreme it can be separatist and divisive, transforming what was once a nation into factions centered only on themselves.[103]

It is a difficult balance to achieve, balancing the needs of the part against the needs of the whole. With excessive balance, history books become bland and boring; yet without any balance there can be no valid text of American history, let alone an America worth writing about.

Eventually, our country may be able to adopt a worthy set of standards and texts for the teaching of history in its schools.[104] If it does, it will have achieved the kind of democratic reconciliation that has always been a source of its strength. Such a reconciliation can only occur, however, if we do not value what we hold separately above what we hold together, for it is, above all, the memories we share that make us a nation.

A Vicious Circle

In this chapter, I have attempted to trace the origins of our national amnesia not to our schools as much as to the underlying premises of American culture of which our schools are an institutional expression. As Robert Maynard Hutchins, former chancellor of the University of Chicago, once noted: "The state of the nation determines the state of education."[105]

Our examination has identified three premises that have shaped, and continue to shape, what our schools teach: materialism, technology, and political beliefs. Over six decades ago, Hutchins, an earlier diagnostician, had identified similar forces: "the love of money, a misconception of democracy, a false notion of progress, a distorted idea of utility, and the anti-intellectualism to which all these lead."[106]

Hutchins also recognized what he called "a strange circularity that affects us."[107] "The state of the nation depends on the state of education," he observed, "but the state of education depends on the state of the nation"[108] He continued:

How can we break this vicious circle and make at last the contribution to the national life that since the earliest times has been expected of us? We can do so only if some institutions can be strong enough and clear enough to show our people what the higher learning is.[109]

The next chapter describes the work of just such institutions.

CHAPTER 6

NATIONAL
THERAPY

America has faced many challenges in its history, and its responses have at times strengthened its connection with the past.

WAR AND PEACE, AND OTHER GREAT BOOKS

Shortly after the United States entered World War I, the federal government asked colleges across the country to develop "War Issues" courses.[1] These courses were intended to teach students about the values, including democracy, they might someday have to defend on the battlefield.

Columbia University's course became a model for others around the nation. In fact, it became so popular that it continued to be part of Columbia's curriculum even after the war was over and in 1919 was made compulsory for all undergraduates.[2] Drawing upon classic works of political philosophy, its goal was to "give the generations to come a common background of ideas and commonly understood standards of judgment."[3] Renamed "Peace Issues" after the war and "Contemporary Civilization" still later, the course educated students, many the children of recent immigrants, in the roots of American democracy, preparing them for "an intelligent participation in the civilization of [their] own day."[4]

In 1937, as the United States struggled to make its way out of the Depression and new war clouds gathered over Europe, Columbia added a second required course. Based on a concept originally introduced in 1921 by professor of English, John Erskine, the new course was based on masterpieces of Western literature.[5]

Class size was deliberately kept small in both courses to encourage personal involvement, and class discussion was led by an experienced professor.

Though the reading lists have undergone revisions over the years, "Contemporary Civilization" (or "C.C." as it's called) and "Literature Humanities" ("Lit Hum") continue to provide a solid foundation of philosophical and literary tradition to stimulate the intellectual growth of Columbia college's undergraduates during their first two years.[6]

The type of education such courses provide is called "general" education. General education is different from professional education. While professional education provides a student with specialized training in a particular subject, general education aims to equip students for life by cultivating their powers of critical thinking.

In the twentieth century there was perhaps no greater champion of general education than Robert Maynard Hutchins, president and, until 1950, chancellor of the University of Chicago.[7] Hutchins's dream was to create an entire four-year general education program based on the reading and discussion of a series of classic literary works, or "Great Books."

The year before Columbia introduced its Literature Humanities course, Hutchins invited two professors from the University of Virginia to visit Chicago: historian Stringfellow Barr and philosopher Scott Buchanan. Barr and Buchanan, along with Columbia philosopher Mortimer Adler, were to collaborate with Hutchins in designing and implementing a Great Books program at Chicago. The faculty, however, rejected Hutchins's plan as too radical.[8] In the aftermath, Barr and Buchanan were hired by St. John's College in Annapolis, Maryland, as president and dean respectively, and immediately put their ideas into practice, instituting a four-year Great Books program drawing upon over a hundred classic works by almost a hundred different authors from antiquity to modern times. Discussions were to take place in small tutorials, amplified by required courses in ancient Greek, French, music, mathematics, and laboratory science.[9] In 1964 St. John's would open a second campus at Santa Fe, New Mexico, built around the same program.

Twelve years before, with the help of Adler, Barr, Buchanan, and others, Hutchins had edited a fifty-four-volume work entitled *Great Books of the Western World*, published by the Encyclopaedia Britannica.[10] The purpose of the collection was to enable all adults who desired a general education to participate in what Hutchins called "the Great Conversation," a dialogue "that began in the dawn of history and that continues in the present day"[11] about the great issues of life. Readers were provided with a carefully designed reading list to guide them in self-study over the course of eight years, as well as a one-volume learning tool called the "Synopticon," developed by Adler, that enabled them to trace the development of certain ideas over the course of human history. More than that, readers were invited to "meet" the authors, to listen to them as human beings, and to share their company through the life of the mind. Only in such a way could these books be kept alive, and, through them, civilization sustained.

Wrote Hutchins:

This set of books is offered in no antiquarian spirit. We have not seen our task as that of taking tourists on a visit to ancient ruins or to the quaint productions of primitive peoples. We have not thought of providing our readers with hours of relaxation or with an escape from the dreadful cares that are the lot of every man in the second half of the twentieth century after Christ. We are as concerned as anybody else at the headlong plunge into the abyss that Western civilization seems to be taking. We believe that the voices that may recall the West to sanity are those which have taken part in the Great Conversation. We want them to be heard again—not because we want to go back to antiquity, or the Middle Ages, or the Renaissance, or the Eighteenth Century. We are quite aware that we do not live in any time but the present, and, distressing as the present is, we would not care to live in any other time if we could. We want the voices of the Great Conversation to be heard again because we think they may help us to learn to live better now.[12]

To Hutchins, the Great Books were not a static canon. As he explained:

New books have been written that have won their place in the list. Books once entitled to belong to it have been superceded; and this process of change will continue as long as men can think and write. It is the task of every generation to reassess the tradition in which it lives, to discard what it cannot use, and to bring into context with the distant and intermediate past the most recent contributions to the Great Conversation.[13]

Our most urgent task, Hutchins believed, was to engage ourselves intellectually and passionately in a centuries-old quest for answers to life's most enduring questions, for only by engaging in such a quest could we fully discover and realize our own humanity.

Great Books programs came to America's colleges in our own century, but the books themselves were here long before.[14] Since the 1700s the Greek and Latin classics had been the mainstay of American higher education. As far back as colonial days, they had instructed our country's Founding Fathers in the evils of tyranny and the promise of liberty.[15] And for centuries before that, they had inspired the thinkers of the Middle Ages and Renaissance with models of intellectual excellence.[16]

In our own day Great Books programs have been attacked on a number of grounds. It is said they are sexist because most of the writers are men, and racist because most authors are white and European. If they are "sexist" it is only because most of the writers of the past *were* men—a fact of history we cannot change. And if they are "racist" it is because Europeans, more than others in the world and with more persistence, dared to explore in writing what it means to be human—an act for which we owe them thanks.

The great writers of the Western world, moreover, spoke not in one language but in many, not in one tongue but a multitude—in Hebrew and Greek, in Latin and Italian, in French and Spanish, in German and Russian, not English alone. One would be hard put to find a more multicultural rabble, always disputatious but united by a common passion to illuminate the human condition they shared. Inevitably narrow, the bridge of Great Books nevertheless is the longest span we will ever have to connect ourselves to earlier places and times. Like all bridges, it should not be the end of the road but the beginning of a farther journey to other wisdom and truths.

Today's "battle of the books," however, is being fought on a wider battleground than sexism or racism. The real battleground is time itself. For today's struggle is a conflict between the past and the present.[17]

Such a battle occurred once before in history. In seventeenth and eighteenth century France and England, scholarly "ancients" verbally sparred with progressive "moderns" over questions of literary taste.[18] Today's struggle, however, is much more serious than a squabble over taste. What is at stake is our collective memory and the effects its loss can have upon all future generations.

Teaching Cultural Literacy

To take part in the "Great Conversation" we must first understand the meaning of our civilization's great books. But for far too many citizens who can read, most books remain closed.

As professor of English E.D. Hirsch Jr. has argued,[19] every culture possesses a common set of terms and phrases that forms the basis of written communication between and among its members.

> Cultural literacy . . . is the background information, stored in their minds, that enables [readers] to take up a newspaper and read it with an adequate level of comprehension, getting the point, grasping the implications, relating what they read to the unstated context which alone gives meaning to what they read. . . . [20] To grasp the words on a page we have to know a lot of information that isn't set down on the page. . . . [21] It includes information that we have traditionally expected our children to receive in school, but which they no longer do.[22]

Cultural literacy, Hirsch says, is critical for the efficacy and survival of democracy.

> The civic importance of cultural literacy lies in the fact that true enfranchisement depends upon knowledge, knowledge upon literacy, and literacy upon cultural literacy.[23]

At the end of his book, *Cultural Literacy: What Every American Needs to Know*, Hirsch, with the help of historian Joseph Kett and physicist James Trefil, appended a preliminary list of some five thousand terms an educated American ought to know.[24] Here are the first twenty-five:

1066

1492

1776

1861–1865

1914–1918

1939–1945

abbreviation (written English)

abolitionism

abominable snowman

abortion

Abraham and Isaac

Absence makes the heart grow fonder.

absenteeism

absolute monarchy

absolute zero

abstract expressionism

academic freedom

a cappella

accelerator, particle

accounting

AC/DC (alternating current/direct current)

Achilles

Achilles' heel

acid

acid rain[25]

Hirsch's list reflected the crucial role a knowledge of the past plays in an informed life: of his almost five thousand items about 30 percent echo the thoughts, personalities, and events of earlier times.

Hirsch and his colleagues would later expand upon their original list in their *Dictionary of Cultural Literacy.*[26]

To some, the whole exercise might seem like an elaborate version of "Trivial Pursuit," but Hirsch is not playing a game. His point is a deadly serious one with important implications for the future of our nation. For if Americans do not know what these dates stand for and what these words and phrases signify, they cannot understand or contribute constructively to the debates that swirl around them. In short, we cannot recognize our communal Achilles' heel, if we no longer know who Achilles was.

Such a discussion is not anything as lofty as Hutchins's "Great Conversation." But if it is a conversation of a lower order, it is nonetheless a prerequisite for ascending to a contemplation of and dialogue about higher ideas and ideals.

Since the publication of his books, Hirsch has carried his educational campaign further by using royalties from his books to help found the Core Knowledge Foundation.[27] Established over a decade ago, the foundation is now working with some 350 schools in forty states to implement Hirsch's philosophy that "a shared cultural vocabulary is a cornerstone of literacy."[28] As part of its work, the foundation has also published a series of curricular guides for parents and teachers of children from kindergarten to grade six.[29]

The Edison Project

Another innovator in education on a national scope is media entrepreneur Christopher Whittle, creator of Channel One, the television service that brings commercially-sponsored news into twelve-thousand schools across the country. After selling off Channel One, Whittle focused on improving the schools themselves by "bringing four big things to the education sector: research and development . . . , business . . . , [the] building [of] the first national school system . . . , and competition."[30]

With the guidance of Benno C. Schmidt Jr., former president of Yale, and other educators, Whittle's Edison Project is today "the country's largest for-profit manager of public schools."[31] The first Edison school was opened in 1995; a dozen were in operation a couple of years later; and at least twenty-five more are to open in locations stretching from Texas to Kansas, from Michigan to Massachusetts.

Edison schools typically feature longer school days than normal (eight hours instead of six and one-half and longer school years too: 200 to 205 days instead of 180). In addition, every Edison family is given a computer so parents can communicate with each other, with their children's teachers, and with Edison Project headquarters in New York.

As originally envisioned, the subjects and disciplines taught in school are to be "intellectually bridged—and animated—by an approach . . . called . . . 'The Greats'":

Great Works. The books, poems, discoveries, designs, structures, and technological feats that are most enriching to the mind.

Great Performances. The musical, dramatic, and artistic works—and the specific productions and performances of them—that the world's cultures have deemed to be of the highest aesthetic and creative quality.

Great Knowledge. The information that is most worth possessing for a lifetime, the knowledge that makes us culturally literate.

Great Ideas. The thoughts, insights, reasonings, and imaginings that have been most influential in human history.

Great Lives. The people—good and evil, heroic and villainous, ancient and modern—who have shaped our world.

Great Problems. The dilemmas, puzzles, and questions—that have well-known solutions, those that remain to be solved, and those that each person must work out for himself—that have perplexed men and women throughout the ages.[32]

The Edison philosophy thus borrows the basic concept of the Great Books programs and applies it to an elementary school setting. Furthermore, the Edison philosophy is indebted to the principles of cultural literacy.

Whether the project can achieve its goals and make a profit while giving students a superior education remains to be seen.[33] Even Edison personnel agree more time and more test results will be needed before they can call their private enterprise experiment an educational success.[34]

Academies in the Making

Besides the Edison Project, other innovative programs have recently been started that draw their strength from the inspiring power of great books and great deeds. In Hillsdale, Michigan, the Hillsdale Academy—an offshoot of conservative Hillsdale College—offers a program from kindergarten through eighth grade (with a high school program already planned) that is steadfastly grounded in history, the Bible, and the great books of Western culture.[35] The academy's motto is "Ensuring the promise of the future through the wisdom of the past."

Meanwhile, under the leadership of Boston University's vice president, Peter Schweich, a new four-year high school academy has gotten under way. The Boston University Academy "provides an education with classical roots for capable and motivated students who live in the contemporary world,"[36] featuring strong sequences in literature and history and required courses in ancient Greek or Latin.

Taking Stock

Of course, these programs are the exception. Even Edison and Core Knowledge schools together number under a hundred. The few Great

Books programs that survive today in colleges like Columbia and St. John's reach only a tiny fraction of America's undergraduates,[37] and Hutchins's fifty-four-volume set is certainly no best-seller.[38] Indeed, it can be argued that as time goes on, Hirsch's cultural literacy list will inevitably grow shorter as a dumbed-down society becomes ever dumber and requires fewer terms of intellectual reference.

Raising the Standards

If these programs, noble as they are, are incapable in themselves of rescuing America from cultural amnesia, perhaps our national memory can be restored by other means—not by a radical change in what students are taught but simply by a determined and consistent effort to do better on a national scale by training teachers better and by designing better courses.

The Blind Leading the Blind. First and foremost, before teachers can teach effectively, they must know their subject, for they are the keepers and transmitters of our cultural memory. The overall intellectual competence of teachers is worrisome, however, and indeed has been so for decades. As Thomas Sowell observes:

> Innumerable studies have shown that students who are trained to become school teachers have some of the poorest academic skills of any students in any field. . . . Students in schools and departments of education score at or near the bottom on whatever test is used—whether it is the Scholastic Aptitude Test, the Graduate Record Examination, the American College Testing Program tests or whatever. . . . William H. Whyte cited a bunch of such studies back in the 1950s. Martin Mayer gave a similar assessment during the 1960s, and a Rockefeller Foundation study brought together still more studies with the very same results in the 1980s. You could go back even further, to the 1920s and 1930s, and find the same depressing results.[39]

This picture was confirmed as recently as 1998 when the state of Massachusetts for the first time administered a qualifying test for prospective teachers based on reading, writing, and a subject area.[40] Fifty-nine percent of the applicants failed to get a passing grade.[41] In response, state officials lowered the passing grade, but then were compelled by public outcry to reinstate it.[42]

In addition to bad grammar and logic, the dismal results of the writing test featured such examples of spelling as "corupt," "integraty," "bouth" (meaning both), "bodyes," "belive," and "bured" (meaning burned).[43] Meanwhile, 63 percent of those planning to teach mathematics failed the subject test in math.[44]

The important thing to remember here is that those who failed the test were about to graduate from certified colleges of education.

These results aren't limited to Massachusetts. In Virginia, one-third of teaching applicants failed a basic skills test; and in Suffolk County, New York, three-quarters flunked an eleventh-grade reading test.[45]

In large part, the problem is due to schools of education that teach theory and method but not content. As Rita Kramer observed in *Ed School Follies*:

The worst of the ed schools are certification mills where the minimally qualified instruct the barely literate in a parody of learning. Prospective teachers leave no more prepared to impart knowledge or inspire learning than when they entered.[46]

The situation is especially bad for the teaching of history. When it comes to American history in public middle schools or world history in public senior high schools, fewer than half the teachers teaching these subjects a decade ago had ever had any formal training in them.[47] In fact, in a national survey, only 16.2 percent of those teaching advanced placement courses in world history had any formal background in the subject.[48] Thus, the teachers who were teaching the most advanced students possessed the least knowledge.

Even if the training of teachers is improved, their effectiveness will ultimately depend upon their own talents. To attract the best and brightest to the field of teaching, teacher salaries must be raised.

In a recent poll, 56 percent of Americans said they would recommend teaching as a career to a family member if the annual salary was at least $60,000.[49] In public schools, however, the average salary is currently about $39,000, with starting salaries about $14,000 below that.[50]

Elevating the teaching profession, and thereby improving our schools, will thus require not only enforcing rigorous standards for the training and certification of teachers[51] but also providing greater financial incentives for their recruitment. Yet as former New York state education commissioner Gordon M. Ambach notes: "Only about 20 percent of adults now have children in school. That makes a difference in the willingness to support education."[52]

In the end, a society doesn't get what it's not willing to pay for.

Giving History Its Place. For most of this century, however, the role of history in America's schools has been defined by two superficial but powerful social beliefs: that the present is more important than the past, and that a subject is important only if it is practical. As a result, since the early 1900s, social studies has been favored over history.[53] Unlike history (demeaned by its critics as "past-ology"), social studies deals with the here and now, and describes the nature and workings of contemporary society.[54] As recently as a decade ago

> a shocking 15 percent of the nation's youngsters [did] not study American history in high school, and a full half of them [did] not take any European or world history courses during those years. Four states [did] not mandate any American history in high school, and thirty-four states [did] not require any world history in order to graduate. Is it any wonder that some of our graduates [did] not even know which side Germany was on in World War II, or that almost half of them [did] not know that Stalin was the wartime leader of the Soviet Union?[55]

In response to such findings, President George Bush in his 1990 State of the Union Address announced a series of National Education Goals, goals endorsed by the National Governors Association co-chaired by then governor Bill Clinton. One goal declared that by the year 2000 "American students will leave grades four, eight, and twelve having demonstrated competency in challenging subject matter including English, mathematics, science, history, and geography; and every school in America will ensure that all students learn to use their minds well, so they may be prepared for responsible citizenship, further learning, and productive employment in our modern economy."[56]

To develop a set of national standards for the teaching of American and world history, a National Center for History in the Schools was established at the University of California, Los Angeles, under the leadership of Charlotte Crabtree and, later, Gary B. Nash. However, the efforts of the Center to produce a balanced set of recommendations provoked the wrath of conservative critics who attacked them as "politically correct" and unpatriotic.[57] In the American history standards, they complained, minority groups had been placated by being given a disproportionately high amount of coverage; in the world history standards, they charged, the proud achievements of the United States and Western civilization had been underplayed.

Two years later in 1996, with the criticisms taken into account, a revised set of standards was published and distributed to America's sixteen hundred school districts.[58] How much impact they will have on education reform remains to be seen. What can already be seen is that the question of memory had become politically charged.[59]

Like personal memory, cultural memory is subjective and in the eye of the beholder: what one group sees and cherishes, another fails to recognize; what is important to some is meaningless to others. What the teaching of history requires, and what the national standards failed to achieve, was a national consensus about what our collective history is—an almost impossible goal when every component of our population is a subjective and potentially emotional witness to its own experience, and when the topography of the land is fractured along racial and ethnic lines.

In the final outcome, the test of history's place in our schools will not depend upon a Great Books program here or a Core Knowledge program there, nor upon teacher certification or even national curricular standards, but rather upon the degree to which we value the past. If we value our past, the rest will follow. If we do not, the rest will not matter.

In the next chapter we will turn from national therapy to home remedies as we explore ways we can develop a therapeutic sense of the past in our personal lives.

CHAPTER 7

HOME
REMEDIES

As I have been writing these words, Gershwin's "Concerto in F" has been playing in the background, the keys of my typewriter competing with the piano's, both instruments driven by equal passion.

American composer George Gershwin died in 1937, the same year I was born, yet today I listen to his music and through that music come to know what he once felt. Transfigured into inked notes on a manuscript page, transmuted by fingers into waves of sound surging through the air, Gershwin's spirit becomes a presence that fills my study.

Once actual experience passes, it ceases to exist. But converted to physical form and preserved, as musical notes transcribed, experience has the potential to be reborn and live once again.

However spiritual or emotional an experience itself may be, it is its embodiment in matter that allows it to survive and become part of our lives again and again. By capturing a moment in the amber of matter, we can preserve it and hold it in our hands.

This, in fact, is what souvenirs are—not simply objects purchased in a store, but capsules housing memories of times once known. As we look at them, they stir our thoughts and allow us to return in our imagination to places visited in the past. Indeed, the very word "souvenir" comes from the French word that means "to remember." In the same way, the ancient Latin for "remember" is echoed in the word "memento."

By surrounding ourselves with such souvenirs and mementos, by inter-weaving them into the fabric of our lives, we make the past an undying part of the present and add body to that fabric . By drawing upon the marvelous capacity of matter to encapsulate time, we can rekindle the embers of mo-ments that would have otherwise ceased to glow, and be warmed by their flame.

Souvenirs and mementos should not be simply packed away and stored in a dusty attic or basement. Instead, they should be brought out from time to time from cabinets and cupboards so that the vibrations emanating from them can reverberate with each new day. A recipe handed down across gen-erations can be made anew even if the paper it was written on is turning brown. A servingplate used long ago by a grandmother, even though its edge is chipped, can be set out with festive food. And a collage of family photographs can be hung, bridging the lifetimes of grandparents, parents, and children. For from such acts we can build bridges across the vast gulf of time, spiritual bridges across which we ourselves can walk.

Mementos need not just be preserved, but can also be created. To do this, film and videotape are only two of the materials we can employ. Diaries can be kept, personal poems written, even paintings made—each embodying and expressing our genuine feelings about the preciousness of life and our part in it. Love letters can be kept too, and greeting cards saved from cele-brations past. Like flowers pressed into a book, flowers whose delicacy and hues can be retained, we can create our own flowers, our own "mnemonic bouquets" to be taken out from time to time and shared with those we love.

By preserving and creating such souvenirs we are not merely saving the past but enriching the present. No life, after all, is lived out only in the now but extends across the years, reaching from days gone by to days yet to be. It is this temporal continuum, this rootedness, that nourishes the tree of per-sonal identity and permits it to grow. Without it, the individual moments of our lives would be like the disconnected fragments of a missing whole.

Such deliberate acts of conservation are all the more necessary in a soci-ety like our own. The electronic speed that characterizes society today can be likened to a rushing torrent, carrying away experiences to oblivion al-most as soon as they are born and replacing them instantly with others just as temporary.[1] A perpetually altered series of evanescent images surges through our brains, pumped into our heads by electronic advertising, enter-tainment, and news. The products we are induced to buy are made not to last but to sell, to be disposable rather than durable. Infusing our culture, the in-visible momentum of this commercial flux erodes the foundations of once stable institutions and systems of value based on the old-fashioned notion of permanence. We are like jostled passengers on a whitewater raft, unable to look back because of the swift current of transience that carries us headlong downstream.

To hold on to our past, to keep it from slipping away, we need to slow down the velocity of our lives. We need to swim away and escape the rapids, for only by climbing onto the riverbank and catching our breath will we be able to contemplate the course and direction of our lives. Only by keeping artificial flux at a safe distance will we be able to impede its erosive force and protect what is worth conserving.

One saving strategy is to dissociate ourselves from the technological speed that envelopes our lives: quite literally to turn it off electronically. Another strategy is to return to slower and simpler ways, ways that are themselves of the past and speak in the more measured cadences of another time.[2] Rather than throwing things away and buying new ones to replace them, we can repair our possessions and use them with care so they will last. We can also learn traditional skills and practice them (baking, pottery-making, wood-working, sewing), not only to make our everyday lives more self-sufficient but also because learning and practicing such humble arts can accustom us to a more psychologically healthy pace of life. If "small is beautiful" is true for ecology, then "slow is beautiful" is true for psychology,[3] for steadiness and sureness have their own rewards that speed, however high, can never buy. In our homes we can give a prominent place to the products of such handiwork—whether our own or of others like-minded—that testify gently to the enduring beauty and serviceability that come of dedication and patience. I speak here not of "collecting antiques," but of cherishing an attitude toward life that things made by hand may evoke. Such "creative retrogression" bears witness to the reality and validity of another time and challenges the facile, but commercially profitable, argument that all things new and fast are automatically superior to those that are old and slow. As humorist Will Rogers once said: "Half our life is spent trying to find something to do with the time we have rushed through life trying to save."[4]

It would be naive to assume that a mode of deceleration is easy to adopt in a fast-moving world. To do so means to swim against the strong current of a society where speed is the undisputed measure of economic survival and material success. But swimming against that current may be the only way to rescue our inner lives.

There are other activities as well that can help us reach sanity's shore. One involves deliberately studying the past. Reading works of biography and history, visiting museums and the actual sites where long-ago events took place, can open our eyes not only to earlier chapters in humanity's story but also to the continuity that underlies it. The communities where we live, our states, and our nation all possess histories that we ourselves are a part of. By learning about their stories we can gain a sense of place that transcends mere geographical location. For time also can grant a sense of place, of belonging, that the demolition of historic buildings and neighborhoods inevitably obliterates. Indeed, by joining or initiating movements to preserve such places we are doing no less than struggling to preserve the foundations of our own identities.[5]

Conserving the past is critical because, unlike factory-made parts, the remnants of time are irreplaceable; once gone, no substitutes can ever be manufactured. Thus, besides convenience and profit, our civic bookkeeping must bear in mind another sort of bottom line that crass economics ignores.

Keeping the past alive can also be achieved by carrying on ethnic and religious traditions, both for ourselves and our children. To have such traditions is to be blessed because they offer us the benefit of living simultaneously in two worlds: our ancestors' and our own. However much the values of these worlds may stand at odds, that very tension can help us choose our path with greater perceptiveness by enabling us to see one culture—the younger one that is our own—through older and perhaps wiser eyes. Indeed, down through America's history from its very founding, it is precisely this kind of stereoscopic vision that has lent our nation perspective. And if we are ignorant of our traditions on a personal or national level, they are there to claim if we have but the will and determination to learn them.[6]

We can also explore civilization's wider landscape, the history of heritages other than our own. This can be accomplished in formal ways, but it can also be done in ways more informal: by reading the works of authors who lived in other countries and times, by foreign travel, by collecting stamps and coins and learning their stories, and by attending concerts and visiting museums to appreciate the music and art of earlier eras.[7]

What matters is not so much the *facts* of the past that are learned, but the *sense* of a past that is acquired—the realization that there *was* a past, one with its own special depth and texture against which we can measure the contours of the present.

We can also gain such perspective in a radically different way: by imbibing rhythms that are remote from civilization's own essence. For, by sending down our roots into nature's own deep soil, we can come to absorb its underlying harmony.

Apart from weather, change in the natural world tends to be gradual. As a consequence, the world of nature stands in contrast to the hurried culture of today. In the artificial world of mechanics and electronics, new models and products rapidly displace older ones. Once familiar objects become obsolete, their places are taken by others that can look and behave in alien ways. In fact, in recent years the rate of technological change has been accelerating exponentially.[8] Nature too changes, but the process of evolution by which species come into being and disappear tends to span millions of years. Even the progress of the seasons is slow compared to society's activity.

Nature, moreover, is governed by the principle of return. Though the blossoms and leaves of trees may fall, ultimately the trees bud again and unfurl vital leaves from the same branches where, months before, the dying leaves of autumn had hung. For all its sudden acts of devastation or its erratic periods of denial, nature's underlying movement is ruled by recurrent renewal.

To walk through a forest, to come back season after season to the same pond and watch the familiar return, is to drink in reassurance, to experience the restorative order of a world that existed long before today's transient artifices were invented and will continue to exist long after they are gone. In nature abides the most fundamental of planetary continuities, an organic testament to life's persistence and durability. To contemplate nature is to experience a different, deeper sense of time—a present that is also eternal.

More and more, however, we have substituted for nature our own artificial world, one in which there is no innate regenerative principle.[9] It is for this reason that we must strive to preserve nature, not so much to save the environment as to save ourselves.[10] For if we destroy that world and replace it with one of our own construction, we will have severed ourselves from a symbol of wholeness and continuity that can heal the self-inflicted wounds of our time.

All these personal efforts can deepen our private sense of the past, even as public efforts at educational reform—described in the previous chapter—can heighten our communal consciousness of history.

However, as we have already observed, the societal forces that even now work to erase the past are formidable, so formidable that attempts to turn the tide of memory may seem futile.

Yet if such efforts both private and public fail, and our nation's long-term memory continues to erode, the future effects of such forgetting will be spiritually devastating.

It is to the prospect of that scenario that we now must turn.

CHAPTER 8

A NATION OF
AMNESIACS

OUR PAST AND OUR PRESENT

This book does not presume the existence of a now lost Golden Age when
all Americans knew the history of their nation and world. As Hazel W.
Hertzberg of Columbia University observed a decade ago:

> In 1880, history and the other social subjects, whether in high school
> or college, were either absent or of minor importance. There was, for
> example, no department of history in any college in the United
> States.[1]

In no way can we speak of a Golden Age of learning when we realize how
few people even attended high school a century ago, let alone graduated. In
the year 1900, America produced fewer than a hundred thousand high
school graduates, compared to an estimated two and a half million it will
give diplomas to in the year 2000.[2] And while the U.S. population more
than tripled in the last century, the number of students attending institutions
of higher learning multiplied more than sixty times.[3] Certainly then in terms
of the quantity of Americans formally educated, the past was no Golden
Age.

Descent into Amnesia

It was in the 1880s, in fact, that history as a distinct discipline began to take a place in America's schools. But the position it finally attained was rapidly eroded in the 1920s and 1930s by the dynamics of an educational agenda that emphasized the present at the expense of the past. It is this "progressive" philosophy that ultimately dominated the country's teachers' colleges and has dictated its curriculums and textbooks for generations.[4]

Our national descent into amnesia is therefore not a sudden fall from grace but a gradual decline that would make a banal tale but for the intellectual opportunities that have been so tragically squandered.

Because academic tests have not been standardized long enough to allow us to compare their results over the course of a century, there are regrettably few ways to demonstrate this degeneration in quantitative terms.[5] Some bases for comparison, however, do exist.

As Thomas Sowell notes:

Some idea of how far this deliberate erosion . . . has gone may be gotten from looking at the once-standard *McGuffey's Readers* from generations ago, or by looking at examinations from that by-gone era. *McGuffey's First Reader*, for example, included diacritical marks to indicate the pronunciation of vowels and the emphasis of syllables. *McGuffey's Third Reader* contained such words as "heath" and "benighted" and asked such questions as "What is this species of composition called?" and "Relate the facts of this dialogue." *McGuffey's Fourth Reader* included selections from Longfellow and Hawthorne, and the *Fifth Reader* from Shakespeare. These were not the textbooks of the elite but of the masses. For the better part of a century, from 1836 to 1920, *McGuffey's Readers* were so widely used that they sold more than 122 million copies—second in sales only to the Bible.

In the early years of the twentieth century, pupils finishing the eighth grade in Kansas had to pass an examination which included spelling such words as "elucidation" and "animosity," defining such terms as "zenith" and "panegyric," as well as diagramming sentences and doing such problems in arithmetic as finding the interest earned on a $900 note, at 8 percent, after 2 years, 2 months, and 6 days. Questions of similar difficulty were asked in geography and history—all in order to get a diploma awarded at the end of the eighth grade. These were not elite prep schools. Often they were one-room school houses in rural Kansas.[6]

In addition, persuasive statistical evidence shows the decline in SAT verbal scores is largely due to the deliberate dumbing down of American schoolbooks.[7] With the misguided intention of making reading less threatening, publishers shortened sentences and eliminated uncommon words after World Wars I and II. In fact, since 1963, fourth-, fifth-, sixth-, seventh-, and eighth-grade readers have been the simplest they have ever been in the entire history of this country.[8] The consequence is students who grow up less able to comprehend the written word and less able to acquire higher learning.

Conclude Cornell University researchers Donald P. Hayes and Loreen T. Wolfer:

> We find it anomalous that no drugs can be sold in the United States without first demonstrating, by experimental tests and clinical trials, their efficacy and safety, while publishers and schools can freely impose simplified readers and related schoolwork on children without having to produce experimental evidence on the efficacy or safety of their schoolbooks (e.g., evidence on the effects those texts have on students' breadth and depth of knowledge and on a major cognitive dimension: verbal achievement).[9]

Dismissing the Evidence

Some would claim it doesn't matter. "It doesn't matter," they would say, "that kids don't know anything. Adults don't know anything either, and their parents and grandparents didn't know anything when *they* were in school."[10] Perhaps, though I suspect many of those same parents and grandparents would disagree.

Even more difficult to measure quantitatively than factual knowledge is a sense of the past. Yet this too must inevitably suffer when factual knowledge diminishes and the very meaning of words is forgotten. As we lose a grip on the past specifically, we slowly lose touch with it generally until the body of that past becomes a fleshless ghost that cannot be embraced.

It is the sense of a past that so many of our immigrant ancestors possessed even when they lacked a formal education. It is that sense of a past that they brought to these shores, often with a deep respect for the importance of the education they themselves had never received.[11]

For those of us who are native born, a sense of the past can be acquired by studying the past. But this activity has also been denigrated by those who regard that very study as irrelevant. In its defense, one writer replied:

It might be argued, I suppose, that this kind of knowledge is inessential to modern life, that it is perfectly possible to get by knowing nothing whatever of history or literature. I would disagree with that argument, seeing no reason why the ambition of educators should be to equip children to negotiate the future with the minimum mental equipment possible, or why children should be deliberately trapped in an eternal present by a total ignorance of the past.

Several teachers have told me that the vital thing in the information age is not to know a thing, but to know how and where to find it out. In my experience, however, those who know nothing are also completely unable to find anything out: They can scarcely read, and certainly do not make a habit of it.[12]

To which we can add something else: teachers have no right to boast they are teaching their students how to think if those students lack a store of concepts to think about and a stock of facts to test them against.

Ignorance and Democracy

In a hyperculture moving faster and faster every day, where ever quicker decisions must be made on matters of personal and national consequence, cultural amnesia is not a viable option if we wish our country to remain a democracy.

As Diane Ravitch and Chester E. Finn Jr. warned over a decade ago:

[W]e can take for granted that the elite will continue to do its best to equip its own children with this knowledge and to send them to schools that furnish substantial quantities of it. But neither our culture, our politics, our civic life, nor our principles of equal opportunity can be satisfactorily maintained if large numbers of youngsters enter adulthood with little knowledge of this kind.

It is on that conviction that we base our reply to all who will . . . conclude that the students did better than might have been expected, that they did reasonably well, that they did well enough, that the proverbial glass is a bit more than half full. It is not just that the complacency of this attitude irks us; it is also that the elitism lurking within it must not be condoned by the citizens of a democracy. We cannot settle for an educational system that imparts "passable" amounts of important knowledge to its more fortunate students while the majority learn less than the minimum required for successful participation in the society they are about to enter. To rest content with a "half-full glass" is to condone mediocrity as well as equality.

Nor need we be fatalistic about this distribution of knowledge. It is not adventitious. It is within the capacity of adults—educators, parents, librarians, television producers, and all the rest—to take steps by which all our youngsters learn enough to participate in selecting our leaders, in shaping our culture, in reviewing our civil life, and in discussing and resolving the important issues before us. One premise of our democratic society, as Jefferson recognized two centuries ago, is that for it truly to succeed, all its members must have an education that will "enable every man to judge for himself what will secure or endanger his freedom."[13]

The greatest danger to freedom, however, lies in freedom itself: the freedom to ignore, the freedom to forget.

Ignorance and Material Success

"But we've been successful," some might answer, "successful in spite of our ignorance, or maybe even *because* of it. That's our strength."

There is no doubt America's story has been a success story. We've gone to the moon, and here on earth have created a society of material plenty that is the envy of the world. Our success is due in great part to our practicality, our ability to do the job that needs doing.

This dynamic trait of anti-intellectualism was evident as early as the years that followed Jefferson's death, when the observant French tourist, Alexis de Tocqueville, came to America. As he would later record:

Less attention is paid to philosophy in the United States than in any other country of the civilized world. Nevertheless, it is noticeable that the people of the United States almost all have a uniform method and rules for the conduct of intellectual inquiries. . . .

To escape from imposed systems . . . ; to treat tradition as valuable for information only and to accept existing facts as no more than a useful sketch to show how things could be done differently and better; to seek by themselves and in themselves for the only reason for things, looking to results without getting entangled in the means toward them and looking through forms to the basis of things—such are the principal characteristics of what I would call the American philosophical method. . . .

The continuous activity which prevails in a democratic society leads to the relaxation or the breaking of the links between generations. It is easy for a man to lose track of his ancestors' conceptions or not to bother about them. . . .

So each man is narrowly shut up in himself, and from that basis makes the pretension to judge the world. . . .

[T]he Americans have needed no books to teach them philosophic method, having found it in themselves.[14]

Indeed, if there are grounds for educational optimism today, they are to be found in the development of our practical skills: in mathematics, where SAT scores have recently been rising;[15] in the climbing scores on IQ tests;[16] and in the growing application and use of computers in our schools.[17]

Yet, like a work of history, a curriculum implies a selection; in the same way a narrative cannot mention every event, an educational program gives priority only to the subjects it regards as essential. And, once priorities are set, budgeting follows, dictating which subjects will be taught and which will not. Because of America's bias toward practicality, and for all the reasons cited in chapter 5, traditional history and traditional literature have largely gone the way of the dodo.

Ironically, those who celebrate America's prosperity may fail to recognize how much of our momentum we owe to the very past we now disparage and to the intellectual values that once infused our schools.

OUR PRESENT AND OUR FUTURE

The Graying of America

To envision America's future it is only natural to look into the faces of the young. It is they who will inherit this country and help fulfill its promise. That is why so much of our discussion has dealt with education, for it is by the process of education that a people's beliefs are transmitted from one generation to another and a nation's dreams are made real.

But it is not into the faces of the young alone that we must look. They are the recipients but not the transmitters of our tradition. For generations and centuries its guardians have been the elderly. Twenty-first century America will be a demographically older America, and the aging of our country will have profound implications for the retention of its national memories.

In 1900, Americans sixty-five years of age and older numbered three million; by the year 2030, they will number almost seventy million.[18] In

1900, they constituted only 4 percent of America's total population; by 2030, they will constitute 20 percent.[19] In fact, by the year 2050, one out of every four senior Americans will be eighty-five or older.[20]

Because the vessel of aging is a reservoir of memory, twenty-first century America will increasingly be populated by elderly rememberers who will have personally experienced long stretches of the past. Indeed, because of the psychological propensity of the elderly to recall the remote past more readily than recent times,[21] these rememberers will function as eager witnesses to history. As citizens and voters, they will be able to draw upon this knowledge and share it with their fellow Americans. And age-wise, there will be proportionately fewer naysayers to challenge their views.

Paradoxically then, the America of the future may become more backward-looking than ever before. The geriatric mind-set of its population may even operate as a braking system, slowing down the hypercultural velocity of a society formerly marked by mindless speed and relentless change.

But of what will the "knowledge" of this elderly generation consist? Surely, we must not imagine these seniors as sage elders transported to our world by time machine from an intellectually and spiritually unpolluted era of the past. Instead, they will simply be the thirty-somethings of today, encumbered by arthritis and sagging skin—alas, no wiser, only older; not more literate, merely more cranky. Whatever knowledge they possess will have been mediated by commercially controlled telescreens; whatever experience, mollified by images contrived by others.[22]

Alzheimer America

And they will be forgetful.

Currently, four million Americans are afflicted with dementia,[23] a deterioration of brain function that always involves memory. Dementia afflicts only 5 percent of those over sixty-five years of age, but 50 percent of those over eighty-five.[24] Thus, its occurrence increases with age, and, as America ages, so will its dementia grow.

Between 60 and 85 percent of those with dementia are victims of Alzheimer's disease.[25] First diagnosed by German neurologist Alois Alzheimer in 1901,[26] the disease is currently the fourth leading cause of death in the United States.[27] It has been termed "the disease of the century."[28] By the middle of the twenty-first century, its victims may number fourteen million[29] unless a cure is found.

Alzheimer's principal cause is not fully understood today, but its devastation to the brain is undeniable and progressive.[30] The disease begins innocuously with random instances of forgetfulness: forgetting where we put something important, forgetting what we went to the market for, forgetting what step to take next in doing a familiar task, forgetting the question we were just asked.

As we get older, of course, we may occasionally forget things. That's no reason to assume we're getting Alzheimer's disease. If we forget where we parked the car in the mall parking lot, we need not rush to a neurologist; if we forget that we drove there, or can't remember where "there" is, it is cause for concern.

As Alzheimer's progresses, the instances of forgetfulness become more frequent and disturbing. Later, it becomes difficult to think and reason, and common sense becomes faulty. Ordinary words sound confusing, and finding the right word becomes hard. The individual becomes disoriented in once familiar surroundings and loses track of time.

Among the most telling and poignant proofs of the disease's effect upon the mind are pictures made by patients in which they have attempted to draw the face of a clock.[31] The clock faces resemble the ones in Salvador Dali's painting, *The Disintegration of the Persistence of Memory*. But these are not the surreal fantasies of an artist. Instead, they are the visions of people trapped in such a painting for the rest of their lives.

The progress of the disease is also accompanied by changes in personality and behavior: mood swings, depression, apathy, anxiety, and aggressiveness. As the brain degrades, it creates paranoiac delusions and hallucinations.

The terror of one patient illustrates the terror known to so many others and those who love them:

One day after a shower, Roy rushed downstairs, still dripping wet and dressed only in a bath towel. He was very agitated and screamed at his poor wife, "Come quickly, Dee. There's a burglar upstairs!"

She wanted to call the police, but he insisted on taking her by the hand and together, even though she knew it was dangerous, they snuck up the stairs to the bathroom. Roy motioned to her that the burglar was inside. He opened the bathroom door carefully, but his terrified wife couldn't see anyone in the small room.

"There's no one here, Roy," she said with relief.

"Look!" said Roy, shaking with fear as he pointed toward the large mirror over the sink in front of them. "There he is! He's right beside you!"

Pictures drawn by Alzheimer's patients

Source: Isabelle Rouleau, David P. Salmon, et al., "Quantititative and Qualitative Analyses of Clock Drawings in Alzheimer's and Huntington's Disease," *Brain and Cognition* 18, No. 1 (January 1992): 77, 79. Reprinted with permission of Academic Press, Inc., Orlando, Florida.

Roy's startled wife looked where he was pointing, but all she could see was her own reflection in the mirror, next to her wide-eyed husband's.

Then, in a sickening moment, she understood. Roy didn't recognize himself. He thought the image staring back at him was that of an intruder, someone he had never seen before, a burglar in the sanctity of their home.[32]

In the final stages, as the brain disintegrates and the body becomes weak and swallowing impossible, malnutrition and pneumonia bring biological closure.

In response to a question, the patient may, near the very end, still say "I . . . I. . ." as though groping for a sentence completion that could lend meaning to the moment.[33] But only the vestigial "I" remains. Once the ties are dissolved that bind the self to an outer world of intelligible stimuli or to an inner world of rational order, that "I" vanishes for all time.

John Donne's "No man is an Island" is psychologically true because the individual who becomes a neuronal island ceases to be fully human. Cut off from the data of the world, the individual is but a solitary prisoner; cut off from the awareness that there is a world, the prisoner ceases to exist. The only blessing of Alzheimer's disease is that victims become insensible to the dissolution of their selfhood.

Dementia and Cultural Amnesia

The cognitive deterioration of America's citizens could be described as a type of national dementia. Oblivious to the realities of historic time and geographic space, and confused by once familiar words and ideas, we fitfully search for the civic virtues and communal values we once possessed but have somehow unaccountably misplaced. Should we not find them, our loss may be symptomatic of a greater loss to come, the eventual loss of our identity and future as a people.

One of the least appreciated aspects of the so-called Y2K problem, in fact, may turn out to be the negative effect of the calendar on our memory, for once we have crossed the imaginary line that separates 1999 from 2000, the experience of an entire century will be "history."

Unlike Alzheimer's disease and other dementias, the amnesia we now have affects not our short-term but our long-term memory. In this respect, we more nearly resemble those victims of retrograde amnesia who have lost the memories of their personal past along with the knowledge they once possessed. But, like Alzheimer's, our affliction may be progressive, eventually encroaching beyond the perimeter of one type of memory to engulf and dissolve the whole.

The Future of Forgetting

It is time to ask whether we can survive as a nation and even prosper without a knowledge of the past. The answer is a qualified yes.

Within limits, amnesiacs can live useful and productive lives, for even when autobiographical memory is erased, procedural memory—the remembrance of skills—can persist. Indeed, new skills can be acquired. For all his indictment of the land of the Lotus-eaters, the poet Homer never tells us it was an impoverished land. Indeed, he makes the point of telling us that the Lotus-eaters were a very happy lot.

Many amnesiacs, in fact, are not aware they've forgotten anything at all. Some will steadfastly deny they have any memory gaps, even going so far as to make up elaborate stories to explain and defend what they can't recall. Before taking a basic memory test, some will confidently overestimate their ability, not unlike the cases in literacy, numeracy, and science tests where those who performed badly proudly assured their examiners they would do very well indeed. Stroke victims will often vehemently assert that their paralyzed arms or legs are functioning quite normally. It may be expected, then, that a nation of amnesiacs will exhibit a high level of self-esteem. With appropriate reinforcement and coaching, such self-esteem could be raised to even higher levels.

Reality Check

But from such levels, reality and its brutal consequences will be hidden. A paralyzed arm is, after all, a paralyzed arm no matter what its owner thinks. And there is bound to be a price for incompetence, however temporarily lucky a worker or a working nation is. We may get away with not knowing when Columbus discovered America or what president dropped the atom bomb, but our children's generation may not be so fortunate when it cannot add or subtract or tell the difference between Africa and Asia. Nature is self-limiting, and soon eliminates the flawed, especially on a planet where others want what we naively assume is perpetually ours.

A Limited Life

Life in America, life anywhere, is more than the total of technological accomplishments, more than the sum of wealth amassed. If we do not know who we are, we cannot fully appreciate what we have. Nor can we aspire to become something more than the things we own. If America is anything, it is not the prospect of greater consumption but the promise of greater fulfillment, a fulfillment defined in spiritual as well as material terms.

The real question, then, is not whether a culturally amnesiac America can materially prosper, but whether that kind of prosperity is enough, enough for ourselves and enough for our children. America's crisis of memory, therefore, is not about the past as much as it is about the future. It is not about trying to "turn the clock back," but rather about setting our national clock to the right time so it can guide us tomorrow.

Cultural amnesia, like personal amnesia, does not enrich life; it diminishes it. As a people, then, we must not choose amnesia as a lifestyle, a lifestyle in which the faces of all clocks are twisted and the human face that stares out at us from the mirror is one we no longer recognize as ourselves.

RETURN TO ITHACA

Ulysses, the Greek hero, never went to college, and he made out just fine. In fact, he never went to elementary school, or middle school, or high school. He never took a course in geography, or history, or math. Poor guy, he never even had a computer, never "surfed the Net"—though he did know a lot about surf, since he was shipwrecked so many times.

What he was was curious. Homer tells us that right at the start. Ulysses was a versatile person, the poet tells us, a man "of many turns."[1] "He was driven far and wide after he sacked Troy's sacred citadel. . . . He saw many peoples' cities, and learned their ways."[2]

Back then you didn't need a college degree. But in some ways that was a good thing, because it meant courses wouldn't get in the way of your curiosity. Instead, the world was out there, ripe as a bunch of grapes. And Ulysses was hungry for it all.

But he also knew you needed a home to come back to. And people to love. And people to love you back. And something to build, something that would last. Like a marriage strong as a tree. Or a son grown tall. Or an orchard that would always stand. Or a world, small as a rocky island, that you could give your life to and make better, make just, make true.

Sustaining Ulysses on his odyssey was the image of Ithaca, "that shining isle where Mount Neriton rises and unfurls its leaves."[3] He carried no photograph with him, only an image etched in his mind. "For me" he said, "there can be no sweeter sight than my native land."[4]

Ulysses' world was simpler than ours, but only in relative terms. There were obstacles and temptations that came in all shapes and sizes. There were villains and monsters, sirens and the unknown. Always the unknown. And promises to keep. And miles and miles to sail before you could sleep.

The Cave of the Cyclops

After setting sail from the land of the Lotus-eaters, Ulysses and his crew landed on a mysterious island.

> We sailed in there, some god guiding us through the gloomy night, for there wasn't light enough to see. A thick fog enwrapped the ships, and no moon shone from heaven, trapped as it was by clouds. No one's eyes could see the island or the long breakers rolling shoreward until the ships ran onto the beach.[5]

At dawn they explored the island. It was verdant but desolate: no human hand had ever sought to realize its potential.

Traveling to a farther shore, Ulysses and his crew came upon a cave and inside found signs that someone was using it as a home.

Later, that "someone" returned—a monstrous one-eyed giant known as the Cyclops. Entering the cave, the giant blocked its mouth with a huge boulder. Spying the strangers inside, he scooped up two of Ulysses' men, dashed their brains to the ground, and ate his victims for supper.

After dining, he turned to their leader and asked his name.

"My name," Ulysses shrewdly said, "is Noman."[6]

No man he was indeed, trapped as he was in a dark cave by a flesh-eating monster. It would only be a short time before Ulysses too would be killed and eaten, before he would cease to exist. Noman indeed.

But Ulysses was determined to save himself and the men who were his charge. So, offering the Cyclops a skin of strong wine he had brought with him from his ship, he got the giant drunk, blinded him with a wooden stake, and succeeded in escaping with his crew.

As it turned out, Ulysses was saved by the name he had used to introduce himself. When the blinded Cyclops cried out in pain, the other giants who lived on the island ran to the cave to find out what had happened. "Did anyone hurt you?" they called from without. "Noman!" the Cyclops answered, and so the other giants, believing he was unharmed, went away.[7]

Yet as long as Ulysses was trapped in the dark night of the cave, he *had* been "no man." Now in the daylight and free, he became Ulysses once again. Somewhere in the darkness he had reached inside himself and found the inner resources he needed to win his freedom. In laying claim to those resources, he had liberated his very identity.

And when Ulysses headed out to sea after his escape from the Cyclops's cave, it was not deeds alone but ancestral history and geography that he drew upon to define that identity. "I am Ulysses, sacker of cities," he shouted defiantly, "the son of Laertes, and Ithaca is my home."[8]

For prisoners of war in any age, surviving has meant holding on to such memories, to images of family and homeland. For such prisoners, even when all else is stripped away, all else stolen, memory alone endures, locked in heart and brain. Such memories have given them the strength not only to endure but to reclaim and renew the love they once knew.

To be sure, there are also painful memories all of us must struggle to forget. Memory, after all, is a two-edged sword. But without a past a meaningful future cannot be found—not by an individual, nor by a nation.

The Song of the Sirens

Sailing onward, Ulysses neared the land of the Sirens, creatures with lovely voices who lured mariners to their deaths. To neutralize their hypnotic power, Ulysses plugged his oarsmen's ears with wax. But curious to hear the song for himself, Ulysses ordered his crew instead to tie him to the mast.

The Sirens did not sing the same song to all the mariners approaching their shores. Instead, they personalized the selection to most effectively attract their prey. To Ulysses they promised to sing of "all the things the Greeks and Trojans endured at Troy . . . and all the things that will happen on the bounteous earth."[9]

What the Sirens dangled before Ulysses was the past and the future: the narrative of heroic deeds to gratify his ego, the prediction of things to come to satisfy his curiosity. Yet it is precisely this twin symbolic lure that Homer has his hero reject.

Homer's reasoning is clear. A daydreaming preoccupation with the future will keep us from seeing the present, just as a nostalgic absorption with the past will blind us to its existence.

The enticement by the Sirens is thus the corollary of Lotus-land's temptation. In that earlier tale, we are told we must resist an all-devouring present; in this one, that we must resist an all-consuming addiction to future or past.

The antidote to cultural amnesia thus cannot mean turning the clock back to an idealized past, an idyllic return to a nineteenth, or eighteenth, or even earlier century that never really was. For all its limitations, it is the present, and the present alone, that we live in and must deal with.

Home Again

When Ulysses returned home at last after twenty years of war and wandering, fresh challenges awaited him.

In the two decades that had passed since he had left Ithaca, a new generation of nobles had come of age. Many of their fathers had died fighting beside Ulysses at Troy, or were lost on the long way home. Their sons had thus grown up without male role models in a kingdom without a king. Oblivious to both manners and morals, they had become an arrogant and greedy rabble, camped out now in Ulysses' palace, courting his wife for the power she held and conspiring to murder his son.

That son, Telemachus, had been but a babe in his mother's arms when Ulysses sailed for Troy. As a result, he too had grown up without a father, unschooled in heroic character and untested in battle.

Ulysses finally returns home, reveals his true identity to his son, and—with Telemachus's help and the help of a few loyal servants—attacks and slays his enemies.

But his job is not done, for the relatives of the suitors march on the palace, demanding vengeance.

In a dramatic final scene,[10] Ulysses, Telemachus, and Ulysses' father stand together with spears in hand to face the angry mob. The scene is fraught with symbolic meaning, because in it three generations are united in a common cause. Ulysses' father, Laertes, represents the past; Telemachus, the future; and Ulysses, the present that connects them. Like a mighty tree—so often a symbol in the poem[11]—Laertes stands for the roots, Telemachus the upward-reaching branches, and Ulysses the stalwart trunk.

The rootless self-absorption of the suitors and the destructive intent of their kin had to be opposed if a just society was to be rebuilt. Thus, in making their stand, Ulysses and his family do not just defend a throne, but civilization itself.

The Tree of Civilization

Civilization itself is like a tree, drawing its nourishment from the sacrifices and wisdom of the past, rising upon the determination of the present, and ascending skyward through faith in the future's promise. Like those of a tree, the parts of a civilization must be organically joined.[12] No tree can live without branches and leaves, nor stand without a trunk, nor flourish without roots. This is the vital continuity that reality demands both of trees and of civilizations.

But reality makes an even greater demand upon humanity than it does upon nature. Trees do not need to remember their roots to possess them, but humanity does, for without remembrance the roots that are our past cease to exist, and without their nourishment the tree of our civilization can only die.

NOTES

PROLOGUE: THE LAND OF THE LOTUS-EATERS

1. The hero's own name conveys the passage of time and how time alters memory. To Homer he was Odysseus. But the western Greeks, who migrated to Italy, pronounced his name differently, leading the Romans to spell his name Ulixes. Eventually, Latin Ulixes became English Ulysses, the spelling I have chosen to use here because of its greater familiarity.

2. Homer, *The Odyssey*, 9:94–97. The translations from Homer, here and below, are the author's.

3. *The Odyssey*, 5:59–74.

4. Ibid., 5:151–152.

5. See the author's 1965 Columbia University dissertation, *A Study of Analogy and Contrast as Elements of Symmetrical Design in the Structure of the Odyssey* (Ann Arbor: University Microfilms, 1966); "The *Telemachy* and Structural Symmetry," *Transactions and Proceedings of the American Philological Association* 97 (1966) 15—27; and "Structural Symmetry at the End of the *Odyssey*," *Greek, Roman and Byzantine Studies* 9 (1968) 115—123. See also Cedric H. Whitman, *Homer and the Heroic Tradition* (Cambridge, MA: Harvard University Press, 1958), chap. 5, 11, and 12.

6. Homer's *The Odyssey* has, however, been given new life by contemporary translations (most recently by Robert Fagles [Homer, *The Odyssey*, New York: Viking Penguin, 1996]) and by cinematic popularizations (the 1954 Italian-made film, *Ulysses*, starring Kirk Douglas, and the 1997 adaptation for NBC television starring Armand Assante). The latter, according to A.C. Nielsen surveys, was

watched in more than twenty-six million homes on each of the two nights it was broadcast. (See Camille Paglia, "Homer on Film: A Voyage Through *The Odyssey*, *Ulysses*, *Helen of Troy*, and *Contempt*," *Arion*, Third Series, 5.2 [fall 1997] 166–197.) Even though they exposed millions of people to the notion of *The Odyssey*—a larger audience by far than Homer himself ever had—these modern popularizations significantly changed the original substance and themes of the poet's story. (See Paglia, ibid.)

7. According to a 1995 "America's Talking" Gallup poll (reported by Bob Herbert, "A Nation of Nitwits," *New York Times*, March 1, 1995, A15, national edition.)

8. According to a 1989 Gallup Organization survey commissioned by the National Endowment for the Humanities. See "Core Curriculums in College Urged" (*New York Times*, October 9, 1989, I.11, national edition) and "College Seniors Fail to Make Grade" (*Wall Street Journal*, October 9, 1989, B1). Though this Gallup survey is over a decade old, more recent surveys demonstrate that such cultural amnesia persists in our own day (see chap. 1). Indeed, the farther we get from the past—even the more recent past—the more it seems to fade from our collective memory (see chap. 4 and 5).

9. The connection between memory and individual identity, on the one hand, and memory and a society's sense of purpose, on the other, was drawn 16 centuries ago by St. Augustine (see Brian Stock, *Augustine the Reader: Meditation, Self-Knowledge, and the Ethics of Interpretation* [Cambridge, MA: Harvard University Press, 1996], 12–14).

CHAPTER 1: CULTURAL AMNESIA

1. *Geography: An International Gallup Survey; Summary of Findings*, conducted for the National Geographic Society (Princeton, NJ: The Gallup Organization, Inc., 1988). Also see "Americans Falter on Geography Test," *New York Times*, July 28, 1988, I. 16, national edition; and Gilbert M. Grosvenor, "Those Panamanian Pandas," *New York Times*, July 31, 1988, E25, national edition.

2. "Majority Flunk *Detroit News* Quiz," *Detroit News*, September 8, 1988, H1.

3. See *Geography: An International Gallup Survey*, 39.

4. Ibid., 4 and 39–40.

5. Ibid.

6. Ibid., 39.

7. "Americans Falter on Geography Test," *New York Times*, July 28, 1988, I16, national edition.

8. Ibid.

9. Gilbert M. Grosvenor, "Those Panamanian Pandas," E25.

10. *Geography: An International Gallup Survey*, 5. To combat geographical ignorance, the National Geographic Society in 1998 sent two-sided world maps to every school in the nation—a total of 100,000 maps. (Reported in "He Said It," *Detroit Free Press*, September 15, 1998, 8A.)

11. Ibid., 29.

12. Ibid.

13. See Kim McDonald, "Interest in Science High, but Knowledge Still Poor," *Chronicle of Higher Education*, July 17, 1998, A22.

14. See Diane Ravitch and Chester E. Finn Jr., *What Do Our 17–Year-Olds Know? A Report on the First National Assessment of History and Literature* (New York: Harper & Row, 1987).

15. See "Core Curriculums in College Urged," *New York Times*, October 9, 1989, I.11, national edition; and "College Seniors Fail to Make Grade," *Wall Street Journal*, October 9, 1989, B1.

16. Ibid.

17. CBS News poll (January 1994) reported in "America's Grade on 20th Century European Wars: F," *New York Times*, December 3, 1995, E5, national edition.

18. Ibid.

19. See Bob Herbert, "A Nation of Nitwits," *New York Times*, March 1, 1995, A15, national edition.

20. See *NAS . . . Update*, vol. 7, no. 3 (October 1996), 4, reporting on a survey, "What Florida's University Graduates Don't Know about History and Government," authored by Dr. Thomas R. Dye, then president of the Florida Association of Scholars. To their credit, however, Ivy League students significantly outscored the Floridians (*NAS . . . Update*).

21. According to the 1994 National Assessment of Educational Progress in American History. See "America's Students Know Little about U.S. History, Study Says," *New York Times*, November 2, 1995, A11, national edition; and Leonard Pitts Jr., "Kids Really Learn History When They Get the Picture," *Detroit Free Press*, November 16, 1995, 6C.

22. Reported by political consultant Frank Luntz, speaking at "The Future of American Civilization," Conference sponsored by the Progress and Freedom Foundation, Washington, DC, January 1, 1994.

23. In 1998 the *New York Times* reported that "most people agree with the statement, 'The United States Constitution is important to me.'" Yet according to the same survey, more than half of those replying didn't know there were one hundred senators. (Nicholas Lemann, "Government of, by, and for the Comfortable," *New York Times Magazine*, November 1, 1998, 43; data compiled by David Wallis.)

24. As reported by Frank Luntz, at "Future" conference.

25. Benjamin J. Stein, "The Cheerful Ignorance of the Young in L.A.," *Washington Post*, October 3, 1983, quoted by E.D. Hirsch Jr. in *Cultural Literacy: What Every American Needs to Know* (Boston: Houghton Mifflin, 1987), 6–7.

26. Ibid.

27. Nicholas Lemann, "Government of, by and for the Comfortable."

28. Cited by Steve Allen, *Dumbth: And 81 Ways to Make Americans Smarter*, (New York: Prometheus Books, 1991), 15.

29. See I. Kirsch, A. Jungeldut, and A. Kolstad, *Adult Literacy in America: A First Look at the Results of the National Adult Literacy Survey* (Washington, DC: U.S. Government Printing Office, 1993) and T. G. Sticht and W. B. Armstrong, *Adult Literacy in the United States: A Compendium of Quantitative Data and Interpretive Comments* (Washington, DC: National Institute for Literacy, 1994). For highlights, see "Study Says Half of Adults in U.S. Can't Read or Handle Arithmetic," *New York Times*, September 9, 1993, A1 and 16, national edition. For reactions to the survey, see "Educators Say New Direction and Resources Are Needed to Raise Literacy," *New York Times*, September 12, 1993, Y17, national edition.

30. See "Study Says Half of Adults in U.S. Can't Read or Handle Arithmetic." The Philip Morris Management Corporation is currently sponsoring the "Gateway: Paths to Adult Learning" program to provide nationwide support for local organizations administering adult literacy projects.

31. Ibid.

32. "High School Grads Unfit for High-Tech World, Survey Finds," *Detroit News*, September 8, 1993, 1A, 6A.

33. U.S. Department of Education, National Center for Education Statistics, National Assessment of Educational Progress, *1992 NAEP Trial State Assessment, 1993* (cited by William J. Bennett in *The Index of Leading Cultural Indicators: Facts and Figures on the State of American Society* [New York: Simon & Schuster, 1994], 86).

34. In addition, an international study conducted in 1995 (the Third International Mathematics and Science Study) revealed that American high school seniors—including the most advanced—are among the most poorly prepared in mathematics when compared to the high school students of other industrialized nations (see "U.S. 12th Graders Rank Poorly in Math and Science, Study Says," *New York Times*, February 25, 1998, A1 and C20, national edition). Dr. William H. Schmidt of Michigan State University, who assembled the U.S. data, said, "Our best students in mathematics and science are simply not world class" (ibid.). Chester E. Finn Jr. of the Hudson Institute put it more bluntly. Commented Finn: "Our 12th-graders occupy the international cellar" (Chester E. Finn Jr., "Why America Has the World's Dimmest Bright Kids," *Wall Street Journal*, February 25, 1998, A22).

35. U.S. Department of Education, National Center for Education Statistics, International Assessment of Educational Progress, *A World of Differences* (1989), cited by Bennett, *The Index*, 85.

36. Chester E. Finn Jr., "Will They Ever Learn?" *National Review* 47, no. 10 (May 29, 1995): 26ff.

37. Ibid.

38. Ibid.

39. "By the Numbers," *U.S. News & World Report*, August 28–September 4, 1995, 83.

40. Ibid.

41. Ibid.

42. Ibid.

43. David L. Littmann, "Business Picks Up Where Schools Leave Off," *Detroit News*, June 16, 1996, B7.

44. As shown by a groundbreaking international survey, "Literacy, Economy, and Society," sponsored jointly by the Organization of Economic Cooperation and Development and Statistics Canada (see *Toronto Globe and Mail*, December 7, 1995, A14). The "good news" was the United States was not alone. According to the survey, "some of the world's most advanced and best-educated countries . . . harbour deep pools of citizens who are barely literate, a finding that has grave implications for the nations' abilities to become wealthier" (ibid.). A UNICEF survey predicts the international pool of illiteracy will steadily rise (Barbara Crosette, "16% World Illiteracy to Grow, Study Says," *New York Times*, December 9, 1998, A10, national edition).

45. "The Outlook: Who Will Teach Johnny to Read?" *Wall Street Journal* November 9, 1998, 1.

46. See Marianne Jennings, "The Real Generation Gap," *Imprimis* (Hillsdale College) 27, no. 8, 2.

47. Ibid.

48. The term "aliteracy" seems to have been introduced by Dr. Bernice Cullinan of New York University in *Children's Literature in the Reading Program* (Newark, DE: IRA, 1987). On the dangers of aliteracy and illiteracy, note the observation of Robert Maynard Hutchins: "To put an end to the spirit of inquiry that has characterized the West it is not necessary to burn the books. All we have to do is to leave them unread for a few generations" (*The Great Conversation*, vol. 1 of *The Great Books of the Western World*, [Chicago: University of Chicago Press/Encyclopedia Britannica, 1952], 2).

49. "S.A.T. with Familiar Anxiety but New (Higher) Scoring," *New York Times*, April 2, 1995, Y15, national edition.

50. Ibid.

51. Ibid.

52. Ibid.

53. See E. D. Hirsch, Jr., *Cultural Literacy*, 5.

54. See "SAT Scores Rise Strongly After Test Is Overhauled," *Wall Street Journal*, August 24, 1995, B1.

55. "A Perfect S.A.T. Score, Even with Four Errors," *New York Times*, July 26, 1995, B6, national edition. See also Diane Ravitch, "Defining Literacy Downward," *New York Times*, August 28, 1996, A15, national edition.

56. "S.A.T. with Familiar Anxiety but New (Higher) Scoring."

57. Bruno V. Manno, "The Real Score on the SATs," *Wall Street Journal*, September 13, 1995, A14. For rebuttal, see Donald M. Stewart (president, The College Board), "New SATs for a New Kind of Student" (letter to the editor), *Wall Street Journal*, October 4, 1995, A17.

58. Diane Ravitch, "Defining Literacy Downward."

59. Bruno V. Manno, "The Real Score on the SATs."

60. "College Seniors Fail to Make Grade," *Wall Street Journal*, October 9, 1989, B1. See also "Core Curriculums in College Urged," *New York Times*, October 9, 1989, 1.11, national edition.

61. "Fewer Professors Believe Western Culture Should Be the Cornerstone of College Curriculum," *Chronicle of Higher Education*, September 13, 1996, A12 (reviewing the findings of a report, "The American College Teacher," that summarizes a 1995 survey conducted by the Higher Education Research Institute of the University of California at Los Angeles).

62. Ibid.

63. "Alas, Poor Shakespeare: No Longer a 'Must Read' at Many Colleges," *New York Times*, December 29, 1996, Y13, national edition. See also "Top English Departments No Longer Require Courses on Shakespeare, A Study Finds," *Chronicle of Higher Education*, January 10, 1997, A12.

64. *The Dissolution of General Education: 1914–1993* (Princeton, NJ: National Association of Scholars, 1996).

65. Ibid.

66. Ibid., 62.

67. Quoted from *American Heritage* (cited by Anthony Harrigan, in "A Moral Redoubt in the Heartland," *Touchstone*, spring 1994: 24).

68. Thomas Jefferson, letter to Charles Yancy (January 6, 1816), quoted in *The Harper Book of American Quotations* (New York: Harper & Row, 1988), 208.

69. George Orwell, *1984* (New York: Penguin, 1981 [1949]), 176.

70. Ibid., 175.

71. Andrew Bard Schmookler, *The Illusion of Choice: How the Market Economy Shapes Our Destiny* (San Francisco: Harper, 1993), 301.

72. Quoted by Elizabeth Pomada and Michael Larsen, *Daughters of Painted Ladies: America's Resplendent Victorians* (New York: Dutton, 1987), 24.

CHAPTER 2: MEMORY AND PERSONAL IDENTITY

1. In this and in later sections of this chapter I am especially indebted to these recent works on memory and the brain: Alan Baddeley, *Your Memory: A User's Guide* (London: Prion, 1996); John Kotre, *White Gloves: How We Create Ourselves Through Memory* (New York: Free Press, 1995); Steven Rose, *The Making of Memory: From Molecules to Mind* (New York: Doubleday, 1992); Rebecca Rupp, *Committed to Memory: How We Remember and Why We Forget* (New York: Crown, 1998); and Daniel L. Schacter, *Searching for Memory: The Brain, the Mind, and the Past* (New York: Basic Books, 1996). For further information about the topics surveyed in this chapter, the reader should consult these works. For coverage of continuing advances in brain and memory research, see the pages of the *New York Times*.

2. For a discussion of the fugue state, see Schacter, chap. 8.

3. Sholem Asch, *The Nazarene* (New York: Carroll & Graf, 1996 [1939]), 1.

4. In Jorge Luis Borges's *Artifices* (1944), part 2 of *Ficciones* (New York: Grove Press, 1962), 107–113.

5. On aging and memory see especially Baddeley, *Your Memory*, chap. 13, and Schacter, *Searching for Memory*, chap. 10. On the strength of older minds and their possible cellular renewal, see Daniel Goleman, "Mental Decline in Aging Need Not Be Inevitable," *New York Times*, April 26, 1994, B5, national edition: and "Studies Suggest Older Minds Are Stronger Than Expected, *New York Times*, February 26, 1996, 1, national edition; and Holcomb B. Noble, "Adult Brains Seen to Replace Cells," *New York Times*, October 30, 1998, 1, national edition.

6. On the value of life review, see John Hendricks, ed., *The Meaning of Reminiscence and Life Review* (Amityville, NY: Baywood Publishing Co., 1995). Also note Stephen Bertman, "A Handful of Quietness: Measuring the Meaning of Our Years," in *Religion, Belief, and Spirituality in Late Life*, ed. Eugene Thomas and Susan Eisenhandler (New York: Springer, 1998), chap. 1.

7. Schacter, *Searching for Memory*, 7.

8. Rupp, *Committed to Memory*, 26.

9. Baddeley, *Your Memory*, 41.

10. For the story of Henry M., see Philip J. Hilts, *Memory's Ghost: The Nature of Memory and the Strange Tale of Mr. M.* (New York: Simon & Schuster, 1995).

11. Ibid., 16.

12. Schacter, *Searching for Memory, 137*.

13. Hilts, *Memory's Ghost*, 97.

14. Ibid., 18–19.

15. Ibid., 138.

16. Joannie M. Schrof, "What Is a Memory Made Of?" *U.S. News & World Report*, August 18/25, 1997, 72.

17. Oliver Sacks, *The Man Who Mistook His Wife for a Hat, and Other Clinical Tales* (New York: Harper & Row, 1987), 41–2. For another case, but mercifully of shorter duration, see Marcia Sherman, M.D., "The Man Who Vanished into His Past," *New York Times*, July 13, 1999, D8, national edition.

18. Baddeley, *Your Memory*, 10.

19. For useful techniques, see Harry Lorayne and Jerry Lucas, *The Memory Book* (New York: Ballantine, 1986).

20. For a discussion of the controversy over repressed and supposedly recovered memories, see Schacter, *Searching for Memory*, chap. 9, including notes and bibliography.

21. I am indebted to Steven Rose (*The Making of Memory*, 122) for this phrase.

22. Hilts, *Memory's Ghost*, 7.

23. For a discussion of the impact of stress on memory, see Robert Sapolsky, *Stress, the Aging Brain, and the Mechanisms of Neuron Death* (Cambridge, MA: MIT Press, 1992). See also John W. Newcomer, M.D, et al., "Decreased Memory Performance in Healthy Humans Induced by Stress-Level Cortisol Treatment," *Archives of General Psychiatry* 56 (June 1999): 527–533.

24. For a discussion of Alzheimer's disease, see Muriel R. Gillick, *Tangled Minds: Understanding Alzheimer's Disease and Other Dementias* (New York: Dutton, 1998), and William Molloy and Paul Caldwell, *Alzheimer's Disease:*

Everything You Need to Know (Buffalo, NY: Firefly Books, 1998). Note also Sheldon J. Tetewsky and Charles J. Duffy, "Visual Loss and Getting Lost in Alzheimer's Disease," *Neurology* 52 (March 1999): 958–964.

25. Quoted by Rupp, *Committed to Memory*, 9.

26. Ibid., 10.

CHAPTER 3: MEMORY AND CIVILIZATION

1. See André Leroi-Gourhan, *Treasures of Prehistoric Art* (New York: Abrams, 1965), and Ann Sieveking, *The Cave Artists* (London: Thames & Hudson, 1979).

2. André Leroi-Gourhan, *Prehistoric Man* (New York: Philosophical Library, 1957), 113–114.

3. Another misconception is that so-called "primitive" cultures are unintellectual. On this point see Paul Radin, *Primitive Man as Philosopher* (New York: Dover, 1957).

4. The revolutionary discovery of agriculture had been made during the last part of the Stone Age, the so-called Neolithic Period. Other Neolithic "firsts" included the domestication of animals, the making of pottery, and the development of village life and the design of rudimentary architecture.

5. Denise Schmandt-Besserat has traced the shapes of the earliest written characters to the shapes of clay tokens used by Sumerian merchants to record transactions. (See her *How Writing Came About* [Austin: University of Texas Press, 1996].)

6. Plato, *Phaedrus* 274–275. The translation is the 1892 version by Benjamin Jowett, slightly revised. According to the Roman general Julius Caesar, the Druids of Britain and Gaul shared similar sentiments (*The Gallic War* 6:14; cited by A.C. Moorhouse, *The Triumph of the Alphabet: A History of Writing* [New York: Henry Schuman, 1953], 161). Though making wide use of writing in their secular affairs, the Druids are said to have refrained from using it in sacred matters, fearing that such a practice would both divulge their secrets and weaken their natural power of memory (Moorhouse). Moorhouse also notes that the Maoris of New Zealand similarly feared the effects of writing upon memory.

7. Moorhouse, *The Triumph of the Alphabet*, 187–188, slightly revised.

8. For the story of the alphabet's origin and development, see Moorhouse, and the works of David Diringer: *The Alphabet* (New York: Thomas Yoseloff, 1960), and *Writing* (New York: Praeger, 1962).

9. To visualize A as an ox, mentally invert it and think of the legs as horns; to visualize B as a house, turn it on its back and think of it as the front of a simple hut.

10. Europe got its name from Cadmus's sister, Europa. Motivated by lust, the god Zeus transported her from Phoenicia to Greece.

11. An early form of syllabic writing, known as Linear B, was used in the palaces of Greece during the Heroic Age, but as far as we know, it was principally used by bookkeepers for the purpose of keeping inventory records of the kings'

holdings. It would have been phonetically cumbersome to use Linear B to transcribe poetry. (For the story of Linear B and its decipherment, see John Chadwick, *The Decipherment of Linear B*, [2d ed.; New York: Cambridge University Press, 1967].)

12. For some of the themes of these poems, see the "Prologue" and "Epilogue" of this work, as well as H.D.F. Kitto, *The Greeks* (Baltimore, MD: Penguin, 1957), chap. 4, "Homer."

13. Sappho, Fragment 59 (Diehl), trans. Mary Barnard, *Sappho: A New Translation* (Berkeley, CA: University of California Press, 1948), poem no. 60.

14. See P. J. Parsons, "Libraries," in *The Oxford Classical Dictionary*, 3d ed., ed. Simon Hornblower and Antony Spawforth (New York: Oxford University Press, 1996), 854–855, and Edward A. Parsons, *The Alexandrian Library: Glory of the Hellenic World* (New York: Elsevier Press, 1952).

15. For illustrations of major works of Greek art, see Reinhard Lullies and Max Hirmer, *Greek Sculpture* (London: Thames & Hudson, 1960).

16. Memory's name in Greek was Mnemosyne (mne-mó-su-ne). The Muses' father was none other than Zeus, the king of the gods.

17. For a portrait of Rome's character, see R. H. Barrow, *The Romans* (Baltimore: Penguin, 1947).

18. Ennius, *Annals*, sect. 500 (Vahlen).

19. For a study of Roman art as propaganda, see Stephen Bertman, *Art and the Romans: Roman Art as a Dynamic Expression of Roman Character* (Lawrence, KS: Coronado Press, 1976).

20. See Bertman, *Doorways Through Time: The Romance of Archeology* (Los Angeles and New York: Jeremy Tarcher/St. Martin's Press, 1986), chap. 14.

21. The crucifixion does not appear in Christian art until the fifth century.

22. The New Testament provides no physical description of Jesus.

23. On the vital role of Christian monasteries in preserving Western civilization, see Kenneth Clark, *Civilization: A Personal View* (New York: Harper & Row, 1969), chap. 1, "The Skin of Our Teeth," and Thomas Cahill, *How the Irish Saved Civilization: The Story of Ireland's Heroic Role from the Fall of Rome to the Rise of Medieval Europe* (New York: Doubleday, 1995).

24. Gilbert Highet, *The Classical Tradition: Greek and Roman Influences on Western Literature* (New York: Oxford University Press, 1949), 40. See also 35–41.

25. For the story of the transmission of the Greek and Roman Classics and their influence, see Highet, ibid. Many of the Classics were preserved through the efforts of medieval Jewish and Moslem scholars, many of whom thrived in the intellectual climate of Spain. Moslem scholars in particular had first-hand knowledge of Greek authors known to Christians only in translation if at all. (See Will Durant, *The Age of Faith*, Part 4 of *The Story of Civilization* [New York: Simon & Schuster, 1950], 909–913.)

26. Will Durant, *The Renaissance*, part 5 of *The Story of Civilization* (New York: Simon & Schuster, 1953), 77–78. The study of Greek was propelled by the

arrival in Italy of Byzantine scholars fleeing Moslem assaults on the city of Constantinople. In that city, the capital of the Eastern Roman Empire, a knowledge of Greek and of ancient Greek literature had flourished for a thousand years after the fall of Rome. These refugee scholars brought with them ancient works never before seen in the West. Additional works were rescued by Italian scholars who traveled to Greece (see Durant, ibid., 78–79).

27. Edgar Allan Poe, "To Helen" (1831).

28. The Chinese had done printing with wooden blocks since at least the ninth century, but because Chinese writing was complex, thousands of pre-made characters would have been required to achieve a truly movable type. (See David Diringer, *The Book Before Printing: Ancient, Medieval and Oriental* [New York: Dover, 1982], 410–412.)

29. Will Durant, *The Reformation*, part 6 of *The Story of Civilization* (New York: Simon & Schuster, 1957), 157.

30. Ibid., 160. For the impact of printing on European culture, see Elizabeth Eisenstein, *The Printing Revolution in Early Modern Europe* (New York: Cambridge University Press, 1983) and, with more detail, *The Printing Press as an Agent of Change*, 2 vols. (New York: Cambridge University Press, 1979).

31. Robert Darnton and Daniel Roche, eds., *Revolution in Print: The Press in France, 1775–1800* (Los Angeles: University of California Press, 1989), xiii.

32. On the revolutionary impact of printing in France, see Darnton and Roche, ibid. For its impact on the American Revolution, see Joseph Blumenthal, *The Printed Book in America* (Boston: David R. Godine, 1977), 1–26.

33. For an expansion of this concept on a global scale, see Peter Russell, *The Global Brain: Speculations on the Evolutionary Leap to Planetary Consciousness* (Los Angeles: Jeremy Tarcher, 1983), and Gregory Stock, *Metaman: The Merging of Humans and Machines into a Global Superorganism* (New York: Simon & Schuster, 1993). See also the author's remarks in *Hyperculture: The Human Cost of Speed* (Westport, CT: Praeger, 1998), 95–103.

34. See Daniel Schacter, *Searching for Memory* (New York: Basic Books, 1996), 37: "The computer is a retriever of information but not a rememberer of experiences. Whether the gulf that separates the two is entirely and forever impassable remains to be seen."

35. George Steiner, quoted in "The Humanities, In Memoriam," *Academic Questions* 8, no. 1 (winter 1994–95): 64.

36. On this point, see especially Clifford Stoll, *Silicon Snake Oil: Second Thoughts on the Information Superhighway* (New York: Doubleday, 1995).

CHAPTER 4: THE POWER OF OBLIVION

1. See, for example, the conclusion to Plato's *Republic*. Another, perhaps earlier, tradition exists in Greek mythology as well, that the dead *could* remember (see Homer, *The Odyssey*, Books 11 and 24).

2. Hesiod, *The Theogony*, 226–232.

3. On this point see Edward Chiera, *They Wrote on Clay* (Chicago: University of Chicago Press, 1938), 233, and Cyrus H. Gordon, *Adventures in the Nearest East* (Fairlawn, NJ: Essential Books, 1957), 13.

4. For the story of undeciphered scripts and languages, see Johannes Friedrich, *Extinct Languages* (New York: Philosophical Library, 1957), and Cyrus H. Gordon, *Forgotten Scripts: Their Ongoing Discovery and Decipherment*, rev. and enlarged ed. (New York: Dorset Press, 1987 [1982]).

5. The amazing thing is that even pieces the Greeks regarded as mediocre are dazzling to modern eyes.

6. See Stephen Bertman, *Doorways Through Time: The Romance of Archaeology* (Los Angeles and New York: Jeremy Tarcher/St. Martin's Press, 1986), chap. 10, and Jotham Johnson, "The Slow Death of a City," *Scientific American* 191 (July 1954): 66–70.

7. See Peter Clayton and Martin Price, *The Seven Wonders of the Ancient World* (New York: Routledge, 1988), and John and Elizabeth Romer, *The Seven Wonders of the World: A History of the Modern Imagination* (New York: Henry Holt, 1995).

8. Oscar Wilde, "In Reading Goal by Reading Town," from *The Ballad of Reading Gaol* (1898).

9. In Egypt, the second solar boat of Pharaoh Cheops has been left in its subterranean stone shaft. In Italy, further excavations have been stopped at Pompeii, although only about 60 percent of the city has so far been dug up.

10. In Italy, the equestrian statue of Marcus Aurelius from Rome's Campidoglio and the four-horse team from the facade of Venice's Basilica of San Marco have been removed from their original outdoor locations. In Greece, the Caryatids standing on the Acropolis are now all modern copies. In Guatemala, authentic Mayan sculptures have been replaced with substitutes at a number of sites.

11. Note, for example, Paul Hofmann, "Pompeii: Perilously Popular," *New York Times*, August 13, 1995, 8, national edition; and Andrew L. Slayman, "Italy Fights Back," *Archaeology*, May/June 1998, 43–49; Barbara Crossette, "Thieves Methodically Strip Iran of Treasures from a Storied Past," *New York Times*, March 15, 1991, 1, national edition; and Judith H. Dobrzynski, "To Save Mayan Artifacts from Looters, a Form of Protective Custody," *New York Times*, March 31, 1998, B1, national edition.

12. Among early practitioners were the Italian Giovanni Battista Belzoni (in Egypt), the German Heinrich Schliemann (in Turkey), and, with some justification because of the Turkish occupation, the Englishman Lord Elgin (in Greece).

13. The Elgin Marbles from the Parthenon (now in London's British Museum) and the gold of Troy (currently in Moscow's Pushkin Museum) are prominent examples. In addition, Holocaust survivors and their families are still trying to reclaim works of art seized from their private collections by the Nazis. Some of these have found their way into the collections of European museums.

14. See James Beck, "A Bill of Rights for Works of Art," chap. 9 in Donald Martin Reynolds, *"Remove Not the Ancient Landmark": Public Monuments and Moral Values* (The Netherlands: Gordon and Breach, 1996).

15. See Marguerite Holloway, "The Preservation of the Past," *Scientific American*, May 1995, 98–101.

16. See Herbert Muschamp, "Monuments in Peril: A Top 100 Countdown," *New York Times*, March 31, 1996, 35H, national edition.

17. Quoted by Alan Cowell, "Who Will Save Italy's Ragged Past?" *New York Times*, June 27, 1992, 4Y, national edition.

18. See John F. Burns, "Pollution Threat to Taj Gains Attention in India," *New York Times*, December 6, 1991, A4, national edition.

19. For the story of the Statue of Liberty's restoration, see A. J. Hall, "Liberty Lifts Her Lamp Once More," *National Geographic* 170 (July 1986): 2–19.

20. Letter dated June 26, 1998, inviting membership in The Archaeological Conservancy, a private organization based in Albuquerque, New Mexico, that seeks to protect sites by purchasing them from their owners.

21. Donald Martin Reynolds in "The Value of Public Monuments," in Reynolds, *"Remove Not the Ancient Landmark": Public Monuments and Moral Values*.

22. See Patricia Leigh Brown, "Hillary Clinton Inaugurates Preservation Campaign," *New York Times*, July 14, 1998, A12, national edition.

23. Ibid.

24. Quoted in *Detroit Free Press*, May 17, 1994, 10D.

25. See Laura Tangley, "Whoops, There Goes Another CD-ROM," *U.S. News & World Report*, February 16, 1998, 67–68.

26. Ibid., 67.

27. Quoted by Stephen Manes in "Time and Technology Threaten Digital Archives . . ." *New York Times*, April 7, 1998, B15, national edition.

28. Quoted by Denise Caruso, "Digital Commerce," *New York Times*, March 11, 1996, C3, national edition.

29. Quoted by James Gleick in "The Digital Attic: An Archive of Everything," *New York Times Magazine*, April 12, 1998, 20.

30. See Richard C. Hsu and William E. Mitchell, "Books Have Endured for a Reason," *New York Times*, May 25, 1997, 12F, national edition.

31. Tangley, *Whoops*, 68.

32. Stephen Bertman, *Hyperculture: The Human Cost of Speed* (Westport, CT: Praeger, 1998), 2.

33. See *The Holy Bible* (Revised Standard Version; New York: Thomas Nelson & Sons, 1953).

34. For most of the information in this list, I am indebted to David Binder and Barbara Crossette, "As Ethnic Wars Multiply, U.S. Strives for a Policy," *New York Times*, February 7, 1993, 1, 12, national edition. For theories as to the underlying causes of such conflict, see Daniel Golman, "Amid Ethnic Wars, Psychiatrists Seek Roots of Conflicts," *New York Times*, August 2, 1994, B5, B7, national

edition, and G. Pascal Zachary, "War, Remembrance: How America Manages to Let Go of Its Past," *Wall Street Journal*, May 7, 1999, A1, A6.

35. Dwelling on the past can also keep a people from fulfilling its future. As a young Armenian says, reflecting on his ethnic past: "Our history is presented to us as war, pain, killing, robbery. We have only had 500 or 700 years of peace in 4,500 years of history. We learn this in school. We learn 2,500 dates of struggles, killings and betrayals. Maybe 10 or 20 or 30 of them speak about something positive. It is very heavy. It oppresses your psyche and mentality. . . . Always 'we were,' 'we had.' The Armenian cares very much for the past and what we had, but not so much about what we have and want to have, and how we can reach that." (Quoted by Stephen Kinzer in "Armenia Never Forgets. Maybe It Should," *New York Times*, October 4, 1998, 16 WK, national edition.)

36. After the fall of Babylon to the Persians in 536 B.C., the Jews were free to return to the Promised Land, where they rebuilt Jerusalem's Temple. Many, however, stayed on in Babylon, where they built a culturally vital community that produced the classical scriptural commentary known as the Babylonian Talmud.

37. Exodus 15: 1–21.

38. J. H. Hertz, *The Pentateuch and Haftorahs*, 2d ed. (London: Soncino Press, 1964), 270 (commentary on Exodus 14:30).

39. Ecclesiastes 3:1–9 (trans.: Revised Standard Version). Though the book's first verse ascribes its authorship to King Solomon (tenth century B.C.), it may have been written sometime between 500 B.C. and A.D. 100 (see Robert Gordis, *Koheleth: The Man and His World*, 3d ed. [New York: Schocken Books, 1968], 5).

40. Yom Hashoah (Holocaust Remembrance Day) comes in the spring on the twenty-sixth day of the Hebrew month of Nisan and follows Passover.

41. Many books deal with the remembrance of the Holocaust experience. Notable among them are Lawrence L. Langer, *Holocaust Testimonies: The Ruins of Memory* (New Haven: Yale University Press, 1991); Geoffrey H. Hartman, ed., *Holocaust Remembrance: The Shapes of Memory* (Oxford: Blackwell, 1994); and the writings of Elie Wiesel.

42. Quoted by Sarah Boxer in "Giving Memory Its Due in an Age of License," *New York Times*, October 28, 1998, B1, 6, national edition.

43. David K. Shipler, "Victims and Enemies, Groping Toward Peace," *New York Times*, September 19, 1993, E17, national edition.

44. Ibid. See also Shipler's Pulitzer Prize-winning book, *Arab and Jew: Wounded Spirits in a Promised Land* (New York: Viking Penguin, 1987), and Ethan Bronner, "Israel's History Textbooks Replace Myths With Facts," *New York Times*, August 14, 1999, A1, A5, national edition.

45. For an ancient portrayal of this process at work in time of war, see the reconciliation scene between the Greek warrior Achilles and the Trojan king Priam in the twenty-fourth book of Homer's *The Iliad*.

46. From Charles Morris, *The Open Self* (1948), reprinted in *The Humanities in Contemporary Life*, ed. Robert F. Davidson, Sarah Herndon, J. Russell Reaver, and William Ruff (New York: Holt, Rinehart, and Winston, 1960), 618.

47. For the history of the term see William Safire, "On Language," *New York Times Magazine*, March 14, 1993, 23.

48. See Arthur Cotterell, *The First Emperor of China* (New York: Holt, Rinehart, and Winston, 1981).

49. See Melissa Mathison, "Where Is Gendun Rinchen," *New York Times*, October 2, 1993, Y15, national edition.

50. According to András Riedlmayer of the Fine Arts Library at Harvard University, quoted by Burton Bollag, "Rebuilding Bosnia's Library," *Chronicle of Higher Education*, January 13, 1995, A35. Well over a million volumes were turned to ashes.

51. Ibid. See also Ivan Lovrenovic, "The Hatred of Memory," *New York Times*, May 28, 1994, Y15, national edition.

52. Roger Cohen, "The Other Balkan Price: Lost Civilization," *New York Times*, February 27, 1994, 6E, national edition. For efforts to replace the lost collections, see "Destruction of Historic Sites Prompts Appeal by Bosnians," *Chronicle of Higher Education*, January 13, 1995, A37, and Len A. Costa, "The Libraries: Another Kind of War Victim," *New York Times*, June 13, 1998, A15, national edition.

53. Kenneth C. Davis, "Ethnic Cleansing Didn't Start in Bosnia," *New York Times*, September 3, 1995, 4.1, national edition.

54. Ibid. On this point see also Daniel L. Schacter, *Searching for Memory* (New York: Basic Books, 1996), 300–302.

55. Joseph Bruchac, Janet Witalec, and Sharon Malinowski, *Native North American Literary Companion* (Detroit: Visible Ink Press, 1998), xvii.

56. Joseph Bruchac, et al., ibid., xvii, xix.

57. On the origin and traditions of Kwanzaa, see Michael Zapler, "The Force Behind Kwanzaa," *Chronicle of Higher Education*, December 14, 1994, A7; and Cassandra Spratling, "A Creative Kwanzaa," *Detroit Free Press*, December 29, 1997, C1.

58. *Sankofa News* (Sankofa Communications Network, Windsor, Ontario) 2, nos. 4 & 5 (November 1996): 1.

59. See Sherry Amatenstein, "A Rescue Mission with a Time Clock" (interview with Steven Spielberg), *USA Weekend*, May 5–7, 1995, 4–7.

60. On the fallibility of eyewitness testimony, see Alan Baddeley, *Your Memory: A User's Guide* (London: Prion, 1996), chap. 10.

61. On Holocaust revisionism, see Deborah E. Lipstadt, *Denying the Holocaust: The Growing Assault on Truth and Memory* (New York: Free Press, 1993); Pierre Vidal-Naquet, *Assassins of Memory: Essays on the Denial of the Holocaust* (New York: Columbia University Press, 1993), from which the title of this chapter division comes; and Michael Schmidt, *The New Reich: Violent Extremism in Unified Germany and Beyond* (New York: Pantheon, 1993.)

62. See William MacQuitty, *Rameses the Great: Master of the World* (New York: Crown, 1978).

63. See Paul MacKendrick, *The Mute Stones Speak: The Story of Archaeology in Italy* (New York: Norton, 1960), chap. 6, and Stephen Bertman, *Art and the Ro-*

mans: Roman Art as a Dynamic Expression of Roman Character (Lawrence, KS: Coronado Press, 1975).

64. See David King, *The Commissar Vanishes: The Falsification of Photographs and Art in Stalin's Russia* (New York: Henry Holt, 1997).

65. See "Scholar Wins Ruling on Nanjing Atrocity," *New York Times*, May 13, 1994, A3, national edition, and Doreen Carvajal, "Japanese Halt Deal on a Book about Nanking," *New York Times*, May 20, 1999, B1, B7, national edition.

66. See Jane Kramer, "Letter from Germany: The Politics of Memory," *New Yorker*, August 14, 1995, 48–65, and Alan Cowell, "Germany the Unloved Just Wants to Be Normal," *New York Times*, November 23, 1997, WK3, national edition. Only in 1999 did the German Parliament approve a plan for building a Holocaust memorial in Berlin (see Roger Cohen, "Berlin Holocaust Memorial Approved," *New York Times*, June 26, 1999, A3, national edition.)

67. See Neil Asher Silberman, *Between Past and Present: Archaeology, Ideology, and Nationalism in the Modern Middle East* (New York: Henry Holt, 1989).

CHAPTER 5: WHY AMERICA FORGOT

1. Frank Bruni, "More Pride Than Crowd for Veterans' Parade," *New York Times*, November 12, 1996, A8, national edition. See also Christopher S. Wren, "Gone and Mostly Forgotten: Veterans Pained by Public's Apathy Toward War Dead," *New York Times*, June 1, 1999, A23, national edition.

2. Bruni, ibid.

3. Bruni, ibid. Honored in 1999 with a Pentagon medal for his film, *Saving Private Ryan*, director Steven Spielberg said: "I think that today's youth have a tendency to live in the present and work for the future—and to be totally ignorant of the past" (*Wall Street Journal*, August 13, 1999, W11).

4. Edward Gibbon, *The Decline and Fall of the Roman Empire* (London 1776), vol. 2, chap. 3.

5. On the nowist bias of the senses, see Stephen Bertman, *Hyperculture: The Human Cost of Speed* (Westport, CT: Praeger, 1998), chap. 2.

6. See Meyer Reinhold, *The Classick Pages: Classical Reading of Eighteenth-Century Americans*, (University Park, PA: American Philological Association, 1975), and Carl J. Richard, *The Founders and the Classics: Greece, Rome, and the American Enlightenment* (Cambridge, MA: Harvard University Press, 1994).

7. Etienne Gilson, quoted in *National Standards for United States History: Exploring the American Experience* (Los Angeles: National Center for History in the Schools [UCLA], 1994), 1.

8. See Meyer Reinhold, *The Classick Pages*.

9. On this point, see Brian Appleyard, *Understanding the Present: Science and the Soul of Modern Man* (New York: Basic Books, 1993).

10. See Bertman, *Hyperculture*, chap. 8.

11. According to figures from the Electronic Industries Association and the Computer and Business Equipment Manufacturers Association.

12. Ibid.

13. According to the Motorola Corporation.

14. See Hans Selye, *The Stress of Life* (New York: McGraw Hill, 1956) and *Stress without Distress* (Philadelphia: Lippincott, 1974); Craig Brod, *Technostress: The Human Cost of the Computer Revolution* (Reading, MA: Addison-Wesley, 1984); and Jeremy Rifkin, *Time Wars: The Primary Conflict in Human History* (New York: Henry Holt, 1987).

15. Alvin Toffler, *Future Shock* (New York: Random House, 1970), 2.

16. Ibid.

17. I am grateful to Richard D. Lamm, former governor of Colorado, for these anecdotes.

18. See John P. Robinson, "The Time Squeeze," *American Demographics*, February 1990, 32–33.

19. Ibid.

20. Ibid.

21. From the "Americans' Use of Time Project" conducted by John P. Robinson and Geoffrey Godbey and the results of the National Recreation and Park Association Survey, 1992, reported in *American Demographics*, April 1993, 26.

22. From the "Americans' Use of Time Project." See John P. Robinson and Geoffrey Godbey, *Time for Life: The Surprising Ways Americans Use Their Time* (University Park, PA: Pennsylvania State University Press, 1997).

23. On this theme, see Bertman, *Hyperculture*.

24. Ibid., chap. 4.

25. Ibid., chap. 5, part I.

26. Ibid., chap. 2.

27. On this point see Arthur M. Schlesinger Jr., *The Disuniting of America: Reflections on a Multicultural Society* (Knoxville, TN: Whittle Direct Books, 1991).

28. Richard Craig, "Don't Know Much About History," *New York Times*, December 8, 1997, A23, national edition.

29. Ibid.

30. Ibid.

31. Ibid.

32. "Students Praise the Three R's in Survey," *Detroit Free Press* (Associated Press), February 11, 1997, 5A.

33. In 1992, teenagers spent $57 billion of their own, and $36 billion of their family's, money, according to the 1992 Teenage Research Unlimited poll (*Daily News Record*, September 6, 1993, cited in *Captive Kids: A Report on Commercial Pressures on Kids at School* [Yonkers, NY: Consumers Union Education Services, 1995], 4 and n. 6).

34. See *Captive Kids*, and *Selling America's Kids: Commercial Pressures on Kids of the 90s* (Yonkers, NY: Consumer Union Education Services, 1990).

35. *Captive Kids*, v. In addition, a McGraw-Hill sixth-grade math textbook now used in sixteen states is "drenched with product shots and trivia about everything from Barbie dolls (Mattel), Cocoa Frosted Flakes (Kellogg), Sony Play Stations, Spalding basketballs, characters and entertainment sites owned by Disney and Warner Brothers and fast-food fare from Burger King and Mcdonald's" (Constance L. Hays, "Math Book Salted with Brand Names Raises New Alarms," *New York Times*, March 21, 1999, A1, A22, national edition; see also Anjetta McQueen [Associated Press], "Math Textbook 'Ads' Flunk Litmus Test," *Detroit News*, March 28, 1999, 17A). On the practice of public schools signing lucrative contracts granting soft-drink companies the exclusive right to vend their products on school grounds, see Constance L. Hays, "Today's Lesson: Soda Rights," *New York Times*, May 21, 1999, C1, C9, national edition; Steven Manning, "Classrooms for Sale," *New York Times*, March 24, 1999, A27, national edition; and Tamara Audi, "Schools Find Something New To Sell: Thirst," *Detroit Free Press*, June 11, 1999, 1B, 4B.

36. See ibid., 20–23. The figures are Channel One's and have been disputed by critics.

37. Ibid., 65–66, where a typical week's programming on Channel One is compared to programming on noncommercial CNN Newsroom, also designed for schools.

38. According to a University of Massachusetts study, Channel One has a disproportionately higher penetration in high-poverty communities where budgets are tight (Michael Morgan, *Channel One in the Public Schools: Widening the Gap* [Department of Communications, University of Massachusetts-Amherst, October 13, 1995]).

39. See "This Year's Freshmen: A Statistical Profile," *The Chronicle of Higher Education*, January 16, 1998, A38–39.

40. *The American Freshman: National Norms for Fall 1997* (Los Angeles: U.C.L.A. Graduate School of Education and Information Studies, 1997), reported in "This Year's Freshmen: A Statistical Profile," *The Chronicle of Higher Education*, January 16, 1998, A38–39, with commentary on A37.

41. "This Year's Freshmen," A39.

42. See "College Freshmen Aiming for High Marks in Income," *New York Times*, January 12, 1998, A10, national edition.

43. Ibid.

44. Ibid. See also Edmundson's discussion of the ethos of consumerism on the American campus in "On the Uses of a Liberal Education: I. As Lite Entertainment for Bored College Students," *Harper's*, September 1997, 39–49.

45. Aristotle, *Rhetoric*, 2.12–14.

46. Such commitment is difficult to measure but is generally reflected in the prevalence of small classes taught by accessible faculty members dedicated to the art of teaching. Another important factor is the existence of a core of challenging courses central to the curriculum. See Charles Sykes and Brad Miner, eds., *Na-*

tional Review College Guide: America's 50 Top Liberal Arts Schools (New York: Simon & Schuster, 1993).

47. Quoted by Mary Corey (*Baltimore Sun*), "Palming Off an Education," *Detroit News*, August 7, 1990, 3F.

48. Surveys suggest 60 percent of high school and college students cheat on exams (see William L. Kibler and Pamela Vannoy Kibler, "When Students Resort to Cheating," *Chronicle of Higher Education*, July 14, 1993, B1f. See also "Your Cheatin' Heart," *Psychology Today*, November/December 1992, 9; Ken Schroeder, "Give and Take, Part 2," *Education Digest*, February 1993, 73Af.; Kevin Davis, "Student Cheating: A Defensive Essay," *English Journal*, October 1992, 72ff.; and Howard Baker Jr., *And the Cheat Goes On: An Expose on How Students Are Cheating in School*, ed. David Schiller (Salem, OR: Forum Press International, 1989). The problem has been compounded by Internet services that sell term papers available from a list or custom written.

49. On the academic sins of the professoriate, see Charles J. Sykes, *ProfScam: Professors and the Demise of Higher Education* (New York: St. Martin's Press, 1988). The sins persist.

50. In two historic cases where great wealth led to the production of great art and literature—Athens in the Golden Age and Renaissance Florence—wealth ("being very well off financially") was not looked upon by such leaders as Pericles and Lorenzo de' Medici as an end in itself.

51. On the history of the humanities and the role of the liberal arts, see Moses Hadas, *Humanism: The Greek Ideal and Its Survival* (New York: Harper, 1960) and *Old Wine, New Bottles: A Humanist Teacher at Work* (New York: Pocket Books, 1963). In contrast, note Aldous Huxley's observation in *Brave New World*, chap. 3: "You can't consume much if you sit and read books."

52. "Men have become the tools of their tools." Henry David Thoreau, *Walden*, chap. 1, "Economy." For a powerful elaboration on this theme see Jacques Ellul, *The Technological Society* (New York: Knopf, 1964).

53. Were all the great books of the Western world compressed onto a single silicon chip, the human race would be no wiser.

54. The original Hebrew text reads: "*Tuv* (goodness), *ta'am* (judgment), *wa'da'at* (and knowledge) *lamdeni* (teach me)." As in the Latin translation, the concept of goodness stands first.

55. See Alvin B. Kernan, ed., *What's Happened to the Humanities* (Princeton, NJ: Princeton University Press, 1997).

56. See George Orwell, *1984*, 1.4.

57. Aldous Huxley, *Brave New World*, chap. 3.

58. Cited in *Detroit Free Press*, February 11, 1993, 10F.

59. For the lessons we learn from television, see Jerry Mander, *Four Arguments for the Elimination of Television* (New York: Morrow, 1978), 323–328.

60. For discussions of history's popularity on cable television, see Bill Carter, "For History on Cable, The Time Has Arrived," *New York Times*, May 20, 1996, C1, national edition; Robert Brent Toplin, "Plugged In to the Past," *New*

York Times, August 4, 1996, 2.1, 26, national edition; and David Bauder (Associated Press), "History Channel Takes Aim at Attracting Viewers," *Detroit Free Press*, May 6, 1998, 7F. When history is adapted to television, however, the presentation takes on the peculiar characteristics of the medium: visual aspects of a story get the most play; complexities are reduced to simplicities; personalities replace abstractions; and emotions outweigh reason. For a discussion of this issue, see Toplin, "Plugged In to the Past."

61. Jane M. Healy, *Endangered Minds: Why Children Don't Think and What We Can Do about It* (New York: Simon & Schuster, 1990).

62. See Charles J. Sykes, *Dumbing Down Our Kids: Why American Children Feel Good about Themselves but Can't Read, Write, or Add* (New York: St. Martin's Press, 1995), chap. 10. Thomas Sowell (*Inside American Education: The Decline, the Deception, and the Dogmas* [New York: The Free Press, 1993]), notes that a well-known high school history text eliminated the words "spectacle" and "admired" because they were deemed "difficult."

63. Cartoon by Richard Guindon, *Detroit Free Press*, n.d.

64. From President Bill Clinton's "State of the Union" Message, January 27, 1998 (reported in *New York Times*, January 28, 1998, A19, national edition.

65. See "President Helps Schools Go On-Line," *New York Times*, March 10, 1996, national edition. For the financial and personal challenges of integrating computers into the classroom see Neil MacFarquhar, "The Internet Goes to School, and Educators Debate," *New York Times*, March 7, 1996, C2, national edition; June Kronholz, "Getting Wired, U.S. Schools Face Steep Learning Curve," *Wall Street Journal*, March 19, 1997, B1; Amy Harmon, "Internet's Value in U.S. Schools Still in Question," *New York Times*, October 25, 1997, A1, B15, national edition; Steven R. Knowlton, "How Students Get Lost in Cyberspace," *New York Times*, "Education Life" supplement, November 2, 1997, 18, 21; Technology Report: "Hard Lessons," *Wall Street Journal*, November 17, 1997, Section R; and Ted Gup, "The End of Serendipity," *Chronicle of Higher Education*, November 21, 1997, A52.

66. Quoted by Tom McNichol, "Computers in Class: A Waste of $50 Billion?" *USA Weekend*, February 14–16, 1997, 10.

67. Ibid.

68. Quoted by Todd Oppenheimer in "The Computer Delusion," *Atlantic Monthly*, July 1997, 45–62, see p. 47.

69. Ibid.

70. Jane M. Healy, *Failure to Connect: How Computers Affect Our Children's Minds for Better and Worse* (New York: Simon & Schuster, 1998), 17–18.

71. Oppenheimer, "The Computer Delusion," 62. In 1997 the chairman of the Texas Board of Education proposed eliminating textbooks in public school and giving students laptop computers instead. (See "Texas May Drop All Texts, for Laptops," *New York Times*, November 19, 1997, A22, national edition.)

72. See Clifford Stoll, *Silicon Snake Oil: Second Thoughts on the Information Highway* (New York: Doubleday, 1995), chap. 11.

73. See Charles A. Donovan and William T. Spont, *Discarded Images: Selected Classics and American Libraries* (Washington, DC: Family Research Council, September 1995), summarized in Charles A. Donovan, "Deselection and the Classics," *American Libraries*, 26.11 (December 1995).

74. With the help of the Internet, computer users can travel back to the cities of the ancient world. (See Debra Jo Immergut, "A Walk Back in Time," *Wall Street Journal*, October 6, 1997, A20, discussing AncientSites [www.ancientsites.com]). Also commendable is Tufts University's Perseus Project [www.perseus.tufts.edu/.). For Civil War buffs, there's the Turner-produced interactive CD-ROM, "Gettysburg."

75. On this theme, see the poetic remarks of Archibald MacLeish in "The Hamlet of A. MacLeish" included in his *Collected Poems 1917–1982* (Boston: Houghton Mifflin, 1985).

76. Neil Postman, *Technopoly: The Surrender of Culture to Technology* (New York: Random House, 1992), 119.

77. Theodore Roszak, *The Cult of Information: A Neo-Luddite Treatise on High-Tech, Artificial Intelligence, and the True Art of Thinking*, 2d ed. (Berkeley and Los Angeles, CA: University of California Press, 1994), 91–95.

78. Ibid., 91.

79. Ibid.

80. Letter to Bishop Mandell Creighton, April 3, 1887.

81. "The Civil War in America," in John Neville Figgis and Reginald Vere Laurence, eds., *Historical Essays and Studies by John Emmerich Edward Dalberg-Acton* (London-Macmillan, 1907; repr., Freeport, NY: Books for Libraries Press, 1967), 133.

82. Alexis de Toqueville, *Democracy in America* (1835–1840), trans. George Lawrence, ed. J.P. Mayer (New York: HarperCollins, 1969), esp. vol. 2, Part 1, chap. 10.

83. *Declaration of Independence*.

84. See Ron Russell, "For Young Spellers, Is Close Good Enough?" *Detroit News*, March 5, 1995, 1A, 8A; and Maribeth Vander Weele, "New Teaching Method Spells Controversy," *Chicago Sun-Times*, June 5, 1995, 1, 10. An acceptable example of invented spelling from a first-grader might be "The ns de sm mr flos gro." ("The next day some more flowers grew.") Russell, ibid., 1A.

85. See Heather MacDonald, "Why Johnny Can't Read," *The Public Interest* (summer 1995); 3–13, and George Will, (*Washington Post*) "Subtracting from National Literacy," *Detroit News*, July 2, 1995, 3B.

86. See Lynne V. Cheney, "Whole Hog for Whole Math," *Wall Street Journal*, February 3, 1998, A22; and Alan Cromer, *Connected Knowledge: Science, Philosophy, and Education* (New York: Oxford University Press, 1997), .

87. See Joseph Adelson, "Down with Self-Esteem," *Commentary*, February 1996, 34–38; Kirk Johnson, "Self-Image Is Suffering from Lack of Esteem," *New York Times*, May 5, 1998, B12, national edition; and Albert Shanker, "Where We Stand: The Smiley-Face Approach," *New York Times*, June 16, 1996, E7, national

edition. Note also a series of essays by John Leo in *U.S. News & World Report*: "Reading, Writing and Recovery," May 23, 1994, 22; "Let's Lower Our Self-esteem," June 17, 1996, 25; and "Damn, I'm Good!" May 18, 1998, 21.

88. See Erin Van Bronkhorst (Associated Press), "Educators See Proof of Grade Inflation," *Detroit News & Free Press*, April 26, 1998, 10A, and (*contra*) Clifford Adelman, "A's Aren't That Easy," *New York Times*, May 17, 1995, A15, national edition.

89. See Shanker, "Where We Stand."

90. See Jeffrey Selingo and Mark Fiore, "Average Scores on Admission Tests Rise," *Chronicle of Higher Education*, September 5, 1997, A68. See also William H. Honan, "S.A.T. Scores Decline Even as Grades Rise," *New York Times*, September 2, 1998, A26, national edition.

91. See Van Bronkhorst, "Educators See Proof."

92. Shanker, "Where We Stand."

93. After Garrison Keillor, "The Prairie Home Companion," National Public Radio.

94. See John Leo, "Reading, Writing and Recovery," citing Robyn Dawes, *House of Cards: Psychology and Psychotherapy Built on Myth* (New York: Free Press, 1994), 243.

95. Sponsored by the National Education Commission on Time and Learning. See Catherine S. Manegold, "41% of School Day Is Spent on Academic Subjects, Study Says," *New York Times*, May 5, 1994, A13, national edition.

96. Ibid.

97. Thomas Toch with Robin M. Bennefield and Amy Bernstein, "The Case for Tough Standards," *U.S. News & World Report*, April 1, 1996, 52–60. See p. 52. To make sure they will be successful, however, greater and greater pressures are being put on the very young. From 1981 to 1997, homework for first to third graders nearly tripled, from nine minutes to twenty-five minutes a school night (see Michael Winerip, "Homework Bound," *New York Times* "Education Life" Supplement, January 3, 1999, 28–31, 40).

98. Laurence Steinberg with B. Bradford Brown and Sanford M. Dornbusch, *Beyond the Classroom: Why School Reform Has Failed and What Parents Need to Do* (New York: Simon & Schuster, 1996).

99. Albert Shanker, "Where We Stand: Disengaged Students," *New York Times*, June 2, 1996, E7, national edition; and Steinberg et al., "Beyond the Classroom," 146.

100. George M. Cohan, "Yankee Doodle Dandy."

101. Robert Hughes, *The Culture of Complaint: The Fraying of America* (New York: Oxford University Press, 1993).

102. See Molefi Kete Asante, "Multiculturalism and the Academy," *Academe* (May/June 1996): 20–23; and Gary B. Nash, Charlotte Crabtree, and Ross E. Dunn, *History on Trial: Culture Wars and the Teaching of the Past* (New York: Knopf, 1997). For a concise statement of arguments in favor of multicultural education, see "Multiculturalism Benefits All Students," reflecting the 1991 majority

view of the New York State Social Studies Review and Development Committee, in *Education in America: Opposing Viewpoints*, ed. Charles P. Cozic (San Diego, CA: Greenhaven Press, 1992), 144–150; and Beverly Guy-Sheftall, "Universities Should Teach Multiculturalism," ibid., 264–268. For opposing views, see Arthur Schlesinger Jr., "Multiculturalism Promotes Ethnic Separatism," ibid., 151–155; and George F. Will, "Multiculturalism Harms Higher Education," ibid., 269–274.

103. The divisive effects of multiculturalist policy can be observed in Canada, where it has been enshrined in the federal constitution since 1982. See Mark I. Schwartz, "What Multiculturalism Did to Canada," *Wall Street Journal*, April 5, 1996, A7.

104. On the standards issue, see Nash et al., *History on Trial*.

105. Robert Maynard Hutchins, *The Higher Learning in America* (New Haven: Yale University Press, [1936] 1961), 32.

106. Ibid., 87.

107. Ibid., 32.

108. Ibid.

109. Ibid.

CHAPTER 6: NATIONAL THERAPY

1. See Lawrence W. Levine, *The Opening of the American Mind: Canons, Culture, and History* (Boston: Beacon Press, 1996), 54–63.

2. For the history of general education courses at Columbia, see the bibliography provided by David Denby, *Great Books: My Adventures with Homer, Rousseau, Woolf, and Other Indestructible Writers of the Western World* (New York: Simon & Schuster, 1996), 17n.

3. The words are those of the course's director, Dean F.J.E. Woodbridge (cited by Levine, *The Opening of the American Mind*, 56).

4. From the Columbia College *Announcement* of 1919, quoted by William H. Honan, "Columbia to Celebrate 75 Years of Great Books," *New York Times*, November 16, 1994, B9, national edition.

5. On the history of this course, see the bibliography provided by Denby, *Great Books*.

6. For the enduring ability of these courses to provoke introspection, note critic and Columbia alumnus David Denby's experience when he returned to his alma mater to read the great books once again (Denby, ibid.).

7. For Hutchins's writings see *The Higher Learning in America* (New Haven: Yale University Press, 1961 [1936]), *Education for Freedom* (Baton Rouge, LA: Louisiana State University Press, 1943), and *The Great Conversation*, vol. 1 of *Great Books of the Western World* (Chicago: University of Chicago Press/Encyclopaedia Britannica, 1952).

8. For a history of the general education program at the University of Chicago, see F. Champion Ward, ed., *The Idea and Practice of General Education* (Chicago: University of Chicago Press, 1993 [1950], and Mortimer J. Adler, *Reforming Education: The Opening of the American Mind* (New York: Macmillan,

1988), xix-xxiii. Traditionally, half of University of Chicago undergraduate courses have been based on the Great Books, but there have been efforts of late to reduce this emphasis in order to bolster the university's enrollment. (See Ethan Bronner, "Winds of Change Rustle University of Chicago," *New York Times*, December 28, 1998, A1, A18, national edition.)

9. See Stringfellow Barr, "The St. John's Program," *Encyclopedia of Modern Education* (New York: Philosophical Library, 1943), and Scott Buchanan, *How We Can Be Taught To Think* (New York: Farrar & Rinehart, 1940). See also Lawrence Biemiller, "Where Students Still Study Ptolemy's Cosmology in Pursuit of the Liberal Arts," *Chronicle of Higher Education*, October 17, 1997, B2.

10. Robert Maynard Hutchins, ed., *Great Books of the Western World* (Chicago: University of Chicago Press/Encyclopaedia Britannica, 1952).

11. Hutchins, *The Great Conversation*, vol. 1 of Hutchins, *Great Books*, chap. 1, 1.

12. Ibid., xii.

13. Ibid., xi.

14. In *The Opening of the American Mind: Canons, Culture, and History* (Boston: Beacon Press, 1996), Lawrence W. Levine argues forcefully that America's Great Books of Western Civilization curriculum is, in fact, a twentieth-century pedagogical novelty: "We are told again and again that until the 1960s university education was ruled by the study of Western Civilization and a canon of Great Books. In fact, Great Books and Western Civilization courses enjoyed only a brief ascendancy: they emerged largely after World War I and declined in the decades after World War II" (p. 15); and "The Western Civ curriculum, portrayed by conservative critics of the university in our time as apolitical and of extremely long duration, was in fact neither. It was a twentieth-century phenomenon which had its origins in a wartime government initiative, and its heydey lasted for scarcely fifty years" (p. 73). In actuality, Great Books programs always had at their core a central body of Greek and Roman classics that had for centuries been regarded as essential to higher education.

15. See Meyer Reinhold, *Classica Americana: The Greek and Roman Heritage in the United States* (Detroit: Wayne State University Press, 1984), and *The Classick Pages: Classical Reading of Eighteenth-Century Americans* (University Park, PA: American Philological Association, 1975); Carl J. Richard, *The Founders and the Classics: Greece, Rome, and the American Enlightenment* (Cambridge, MA: Harvard University Press, 1994); and Susan Ford Wiltshire, *Greece, Rome, and the Bill of Rights* (Norman, OK: University of Oklahoma Press, 1992). Note also Joseph Plescia, *The Bill of Rights and Roman Law: A Comparative Study* (Bethesda, MD: Austin & Winfield, 1995).

16. For surveys of the impact of the Classics on later ages, see Gilbert Highet, *The Classical Tradition: Greek and Roman Influences on Western Literature* (New York: Oxford University Press, 1949, 1953), and Moses Hadas, *Humanism: The Greek Ideal and Its Survival* (New York: Harper, 1960).

17. See Stephen Bertman, *Hyperculture: The Human Cost of Speed* (Westport, CT: Praeger, 1998).

18. For a discussion of the "Battle of the Books," see Highet, *The Classical Tradition*, chap. 14.

19. See Hirsch's *Cultural Literacy: What Every American Needs to Know* (New York: Random House, 1988), and *The Schools We Need; And Why We Don't Have Them* (New York: Doubleday, 1996).

20. Hirsch, *Cultural Literacy*, 2.

21. Ibid., 3.

22. Ibid., 19.

23. Ibid., 12.

24. Ibid., 146–215.

25. Ibid., 152.

26. E.D. Hirsch Jr., Joseph F. Kett, and James Trefil, *The Dictionary of Cultural Literacy* (2d ed. rev. and updated; Boston: Houghton Mifflin, 1993).

27. The foundation is based in Charlottesville, Virginia.

28. From Thomas Toch, "Schools That Work," *U.S. News & World Report*, October 7, 1996, 58–64.

29. For the complete current list of curricular guides see the entries under Hirsch in this work's Recommended Reading. New volumes may be added in the future. See also John Holdren and E. D. Hirsch, Jr., *Books to Build On: A Grade-by-Grade Resource Guide for Parents and Teachers* (New York: Dell, 1996).

30. Christopher Whittle, from "The Education of Chris Whittle," *Psychology Today*, September/October 1997, 31.

31. Peggy Walsh-Sarnecki, "For-Profit School Offers More Choice," *Detroit Free Press*, May 29, 1998, 3B.

32. Letter to the author dated September 3, 1993, from Nancy Young, Director, Media Relations, The Edison Project.

33. The Edison Project has received new funding that will enable it to expand further. See "Whittle's Schools Getting Investor Infusion," *New York Times*, January 7, 1998, C4, national edition; and "New Financing to Allow Edison to Expand," *Wall Street Journal*, January 7, 1998, A6. To make a profit, it must educate each student at a cost lower than the amount it receives per pupil from the school district in which it operates. For a critique of for-profit education management, see Phyllis Vine, "To Market, To Market...The School Business Sells Kids Short," *The Nation*, September 8, 1997, 11ff.

34. See Peter Applebome, "Grading For-Profit Schools: So Far, So Good," *New York Times*, June 26, 1996, 1, national edition; and Jacques Steinberg, "Edison Schools Unimpressive, Union Asserts," *New York Times*, May 8, 1996, A15, national edition. In the latter article, Edison officials are quoted as agreeing that at least five years worth of data will be needed before they can assess the success of their program.

35. See Robert C. Hanna, "The Hillsdale Academy: A Model for America," *Imprimis* (Hillsdale College), June 1997, 5–8; and Thomas Sowell, "Hillsdale Bucks Educational Faddists," *Detroit News*, September 24, 1995, 15A.

36. See Sean O'Rourke, "Boston University Makes Classics Basis for New Four-Year Secondary Academy," American Classical League *Newsletter*, winter 1996, 8–9.

37. According to *Barron's Profiles of American Colleges*, 22d ed. (Hauppauge, NY: Barron's Educational Services, 1997), fewer than four thousand students are enrolled in Columbia College and fewer than one thousand at St. John's College (when Annapolis and Santa Fe enrollments are combined). The number of students attending four-year colleges and universities in the United States currently totals about 8,800,000.

38. According to Gary Schoepfel, director of adult programs for the Chicago-based Great Books Foundation, membership in Great Books reading clubs has dropped from a high of 40,000 in the 1960s to between fifteen-thousand and twenty-thousand today. (See Eileen Daspin, "The Tyranny of the Book Group," *Wall Street Journal*, January 15, 1999, W4.) The study of the Great Books has, however, been given new vigor by the work of the Center for the Study of The Great Ideas, cofounded by Mortimer J. Adler and Max Weismann. The Center publishes an e-journal and sponsors on-line seminars for its members to participate in. For further information, see the Center's Web Site: www.TheGreat-Ideas.org.

39. Thomas Sowell, "Teaching Empire Strikes Back with an Ignorance about Facts," *Detroit News*, January 14, 1996, 13A.

40. See John Silber, "Those Who Can't Teach," *New York Times*, July 7, 1998, A19, national edition; Robert J. Samuelson, "The Wastage in Education," *Newsweek*, August 10, 1998, 49; and John Leo, "Dumbing Down Teachers," *U.S. News & World Report*, August 3, 1998, 15.

41. The passing grade for prospective teachers was 77 (C+), a not unreasonable grade considering their future responsibilities.

42. See Sandra Feldman (president, American Federation of Teachers), "Ignoring Standards," *New York Times*, August 2, 1998, 7 WK, national edition.

43. See Silber, "Those Who Can't Teach."

44. Ibid.

45. See Garry Wills, "Teachers Should Take Tests, Too," *Detroit Free Press*, July 20, 1998, 7A.

46. Rita Kramer, *Ed School Follies: The Miseducation of America's Teachers* (New York: Free Press, 1991), 220. On the challenges of teacher education see three articles in *Academe* 85, no. 1 (January/February 1999): Linda Darling-Hammond, "Educating Teachers: The Academy's Greatest Failure or Its Most Important Future?" (26–33); David F. Labaree, "Too Easy a Target: The Trouble with Ed Schools and the Implications for the University" (34–39); and Frances Maher and Mary Kay Tetreault, "Knowledge Versus Pedagogy: The Marginalization of Teacher Education" (40–43).

47. See David O'Shea, *Implementing the American History Curriculum in Public Middle Schools* (Los Angeles: National Center for History in the Schools [UCLA], 1994), 20, and *Implementing the World History Curriculum in Public*

Senior High Schools (Los Angeles: National Center for History in the Schools [UCLA], 1994), 29.

48. O'Shea, *Implementing the World History Curriculum in Public Senior High Schools*, 29.

49. Randall C. Archibold, "Students' Success Depends On Teachers Most, Poll Says," *New York Times*, November 18, 1998, C24, national edition.

50. Steven Greenhouse, "Adding Up the Impact of Raising Salaries," *New York Times*, August 8, 1999, 16WK, national edition. Greenhouse provides a good summary of the debate over whether higher salaries promote better teaching.

51. For steps being taken, see Kit Lively, "States Move to Toughen Standards for Teacher-Education Programs," *Chronicle of Higher Education*, July 31, 1998, A27, and Ethan Bronner, "Teachers Pursuing Quality Control," *New York Times*, July 20, 1998, A13, national edition.

52. Archibold, "Students' Success Depends on Teachers."

53. See Hazel W. Hertzberg, "History and Progressivism: A Century of Reform Proposals," in *Historical Literacy: The Case for History in American Education*, ed. Paul Gagnon (Boston: Houghton Mifflin, 1989), chap. 4. Also, Diane Ravitch, "The Plight of History in American Schools," in Gagnon, *Historical Literacy*, chap. 3.

54. Ibid.

55. Kenneth T. Jackson and Barbara B. Jackson, "Why the Time is Right to Reform the History Curriculum," in Gagnon, *Historical Literacy*, 11.

56. See Gary B. Nash, Charlotte Crabtree, and Ross E. Dunn, *History on Trial: Culture Wars and the Teaching of the Past* (New York: Knopf, 1997), 274, and David O'Shea, *Implementing the American History Curriculum in Public Senior High Schools* (Los Angeles: National Center for History in the Schools, [UCLA] 1994), 110–111, 150.

57. Nash et al., *History on Trial*, chap. 1 and 8.

58. Ibid., 258.

59. Ibid., chap. 10.

CHAPTER 7: HOME REMEDIES

1. On this subject see Stephen Bertman, *Hyperculture: The Human Cost of Speed* (Westport, CT: Praeger, 1998).

2. Ibid., chap. 9. See also David Shi, *The Simple Life: Plain Living and High Thinking in American Culture* (New York: Oxford University Press, 1986); Duane Elgin, *Voluntary Simplicity: Toward a Way of Life That is Outwardly Simple, Inwardly Rich* (New York: Morrow, 1981): Joe Dominguez and Vicki Robin, *Your Money or Your Life: Transforming Your Relationship with Money and Achieving Financial Independence* (New York: Viking Penguin, 1992); and Adair Lara, *Slowing Down in a Speeded-Up World* (Berkeley, CA: Conari Press, 1994).

3. I am grateful to author Jerry Mander for this concept (1993 interview).

4. Will Rogers, *The Autobiography of Will Rogers* (New York: AMS Press, 1976 [1949]), 15.

5. Among the national organizations spearheading this effort are the National Trust for Historic Preservation in Washington, DC, and the Archaeological Conservancy in Albuquerque, New Mexico.

6. For a valuable introduction to America's past see Paul Johnson's *A History of the American People* (New York: HarperCollins, 1997).

7. For an eloquent survey of Western and Oriental civilization see Will and Ariel Durant's multivolume *The Story of Civilization* (New York: Simon & Schuster, 1954–1965). See also Stephen Bertman, *Doorways Through Time: The Romance of Archaeology* (Los Angeles and New York: Jeremy Tarcher/St. Martin's Press, 1986).

8. See my discussion in chap. 5. For further evidence of the acceleration of American society, see Bertman, *Hyperculture*, especially chap. 1.

9. See *Hyperculture*, chap. 8.

10. One of the national leaders in this effort is the San Francisco-based Sierra Club. But our own local efforts are just as important.

CHAPTER 8: A NATION OF AMNESIACS

1. Hazel W. Hertzberg, "History and Progressivism: A Century of Reform Proposals," in *Historical Literacy: The Case for History in American Education*, ed. Paul Gagnon (Boston: Houghton Mifflin, 1989), 70. Hertzberg points out that "history was usually attached to the classics and ancient languages."

2. Source: U.S. Department of Education, National Center for Education Statistics (see Borgna Brunner, ed., *1998 Information Please Almanac* [Boston: Information Please, 1997], 861).

3. Source: U.S. Department of Education (see Robert Famighetti, et al., eds., *The World Almanac and Book of Facts, 1998* [Mahwah, NJ: World Almanac Books, 1997], 220).

4. See Hertzberg, "History and Progressivism," 69–99; and Gary B. Nash, Charlotte Crabtree, and Ross E. Dunn, *History on Trial: Culture Wars and the Teaching of the Past* (New York: Knopf, 1997), chap. 2. Notable exceptions have been the states of California and Virginia, where rigorous history standards for schools have been instituted.

5. This difficulty was noted over a decade ago by Diane Ravitch and Chester E. Finn Jr. in *What Do Our 17–Year-Olds Know? A Report on the First National Assessment of History and Literature* (New York: Harper & Row, 1987), 200.

6. Thomas Sowell, *Inside American Education: The Decline, the Deception, the Dogmas* (New York, Free Press, 1993), 7–8. Another remarkable example is the historical density of the *New York Times* editorial published on the eve of the twentieth century (*New York Times*, December 31, 1899, 20). High educational standards in our country are also evident in autobiographical and semi-autobiographical literary works (by Laura Ingalls Wilder, Lucy Johnston Sypher, and Maud Hart Lovelace) describing childhood and schooling in the Midwest

during the late nineteenth and early twentieth centuries. (For this fact I am indebted to Susan Wendt-Hildebrandt.)

7. See Donald P. Hayes, Loreen T. Wolfer, and Michael F. Wolfe, "Schoolbook Simplification and Its Relation to the Decline in SAT-Verbal Scores," *American Educational Research Journal* 33, no. 2 (summer 1996): 489–508. See also Jeanne S. Chall, "An Analysis of Textbooks in Relation to Declining SAT Scores" (Report of the Advisory Panel on the Scholastic Aptitude Test Score Decline: Appendices to On Further Examination) (New York: College Board, 1977).

8. On these points, see Hayes, Wolfer, and Wolfe, "Schoolbook Simplification."

9. Hayes et al., ibid., 506. Gilbert T. Sewall and Stapley W. Emberling ("A New Generation of History Textbooks," *Social Science and Modern Society* 36, no. 1 [November/December 1998]: 78–82) note especially the alarming trend among textbook publishers to truncate text and substitute pictures for words.

10. Adapted from remarks made to the author by Diane Ravitch, characterizing the critics who attacked her book, *What Do Our 17-Year-Olds Know?* (e-mail, November 30, 1998).

11. My mother tells me that, upon learning I had passed my doctoral oral, my father, who had never completed high school, wept.

12. Theodore Dalrymple, "And You Thought American Schools Were Bad," *Wall Street Journal*, December 9, 1998, A22. Dalrymple's remarks—about English schools—have transatlantic relevance.

13. Diane Ravitch and Chester E. Finn Jr., *What Do Our 17-Year-Olds Know?*, 252.

14. Alexis de Tocqueville, *Democracy in America*, trans. George Lawrence, ed. J. P. Mayer (New York: Harper & Row, 1969), see esp. vol. 2, part 1, chap. 1, 429–430. On this theme see Richard Hofstadter, *Anti-Intellectualism in American Life* (New York: Random House, 1966).

15. See Peter Applebome, "National Tests Show Gains in Math for U.S. Students in Three Grades," *New York Times*, February 28, 1997, A9, national edition; and "Students' Test Scores Show Slow but Steady Gains at Nation's Schools," *New York Times*, September 3, 1997, A17, national edition.

16. See Trish Hall, "I.Q. Scores Are Up, and Psychologists Wonder Why," *New York Times*, February 24, 1998, B11–12, national edition; and Ulrich Neisser, ed., *The Rising Curve: Long-Term Gains in I.Q. and Related Measures* (Washington, DC: American Psychological Association, 1998). Wendy M. Williams of Cornell University suggests that "fluid intelligence, or the ability to know how to do something, is growing while crystallized intelligence, the possession of information, is decreasing" (reported by Hall, "I.Q. Scores Are Up,", B12).

17. It is wrong, however, to have blind faith in the computer as the source of our pedagogical salvation. On this issue, see Jane M. Healy, *Failure to Connect: How Computers Affect Our Children's Minds—for Better and Worse* (New York:

Simon & Schuster, 1998), esp. chap. 1, "Blundering Into the Future: Hype and Hope."

18. Source: U.S. Bureau of Census (see John W. Wright, ed., *The New York Times 1998 Almanac* [New York: Penguin Putnam, 1997], 276.)

19. Ibid.

20. Ibid.

21. On this propensity and its positive potential, see Daniel L. Schacter, *Searching for Memory: The Brain, the Mind, and the Past* (New York: Basic Books, 1996), chap. 3 and 10.

22. On this point see Stephen Bertman, *Hyperculture: The Human Cost of Speed* (Westport, CT: Praeger, 1998), 78–80. For a completely opposite and optimistic projection, see Theodore Roszak, *America the Wise: The Longevity Revolution and the True Wealth of Nations* (New York: Houghton Mifflin, 1998).

23. Muriel R. Gillick, *Tangled Minds: Understanding Alzheimer's Disease and Other Dementias* (New York: Dutton, 1998), 3.

24. Ibid.

25. Ibid. (60 to 70 percent); William Molloy and Paul Caldwell, *Alzheimer's Disease: Everything You Need to Know* (Buffalo, NY: Firefly Books, 1998), 5 and 135 (60 to 75 percent).

26. For an account of its discovery, see Molloy and Caldwell, chap. 1.

27. Ibid., 13.

28. Gillick, *Tangled Minds*, 3. Gillick notes this description was first applied to the disease by Lewis Thomas, *Late Night Thoughts on Listening to Mahler's Ninth Symphony* (New York: Viking, 1983).

29. According to a projection by the Alzheimer's Association (see the chart, "The Alzheimer Explosion," in the *Wall Street Journal*, November 16, 1998, B8).

30. For theories of causation see Gillick, *Tangled Minds*, chap. 2, and Molloy and Caldwell, *Alzheimer's Disease*, chap. 8.

31. Isabelle Rouleau, David P. Salmon, et al., "Quantitative and Qualitative Analyses of Clock Drawings in Alzheimer's and Huntington's Disease," *Brain and Cognition* 18, no. 1 (January 1992): 70–87, and Molloy and Caldwell, *Alzheimer's Disease*, 62.

32. Ibid., 55–56.

33. Gillick, *Tangled Minds*, 225.

EPILOGUE: RETURN TO ITHACA

1. *The Odyssey* 1:1.

2. Ibid., 1:2–3.

3. Ibid., 9:21–22.

4. Ibid., 9:27–28.

5. Ibid., 9:142–148.

6. Ibid., 9:366–367.

7. Ibid., 9:399–414.

8. Ibid., 9:504–505.

9. Ibid., 12:189–191.

10. Ibid., 24:492ff.

11. When the sleeping Ulysses is brought home to Ithaca on a Phaeacian ship, the sailors set his body down near an olive tree (*The Odyssey* 13:96–125). Significantly, the olive tree in Greek religion was sacred to Athena, the goddess of the intellect who served as Ulysses' protector.

Later in the story, trees become the device by which Ulysses reveals his identity to his wife and his father. He describes to Penelope how he carved the wood of their marriage bed with his own hands, hewing the bedpost from an olive tree that grew in the courtyard of their palace and was still firmly rooted there (ibid., 23:173–206). Later, he reveals his identity to Laertes by naming and numbering the fruit trees his father had long ago promised to give him (ibid., 24:327–348). In each case, a memory becomes the key to unlocking the present.

In this connection, see Howard Porter's discussion of the symbolism of the olive tree in *The Odyssey* (Homer, *The Odyssey*, trans. George Herbert Palmer, ed. Howard Porter [New York: Bantam, 1962] 5–6.)

12. In this connection, note the concept of generativity advanced by psychologist Erik H. Erikson (in *Childhood and Society*, 2d ed. [New York: Norton, 1963], 266–268, and *Insight and Responsibility* [New York: Norton, 1964], 130–132). I am grateful to John Kotre for calling this to my attention. For further discussion of generativity, see Dan P. McAdams and Ed de St. Aubin, eds., *Generativity and Adult Development: How and Why We Care for the Next Generation* (Washington, D.C.: American Psychological Association, 1998), esp. 15–16.

RECOMMENDED READING

PERSONAL MEMORY

Baddeley, Alan. *Your Memory: A User's Guide*. London: Prion, 1996.

Bjork, Elizabeth Ligon, and Robert A., eds. *Memory*. Los Angeles: University of California Press, 1996.

Campbell, Jeremy. *The Improbable Machine: What New Discoveries in Artificial Intelligence Reveal about the Mind*. New York: Simon & Schuster, 1985.

Chalmers, David J. *The Conscious Mind: In Search of a Fundamental Theory*. New York: Oxford University Press, 1996.

Churchland, Paul M. *The Engine of Reason, the Seat of the Soul: A Philosophical Journey into the Brain*. Cambridge, MA: MIT Press, 1993.

Crick, Francis. *The Astonishing Hypothesis: The Scientific Search for the Soul*. New York: Scribner's, 1994.

Crook, Thomas H., III. *Memory Cure*. New York: Pocket Books, 1998.

Damasio, Antonio R. *Descartes' Error: Emotion, Reason, and the Human Brain*. New York: Grosset/Putnam, 1995.

DeFelice, Stephen, and Sue Nirenberg. *Memory Loss: Normal vs. Abnormal*. Secaucus, NJ: Lyle Stuart, 1987.

Dennett, Daniel C. *Consciousness Explained*. Boston: Little, Brown, 1992.

——— . *Kinds of Minds: Toward an Understanding of Consciousness*. New York: Basic Books, 1996.

Donaldson, Margaret. *Human Minds: An Exploration*. New York: Penguin, 1992.

Fischbach, Gerald D., et al. "Mind and Brain" (Special Issue), *Scientific American*, September 1992.

Freedman, David. *Brainmakers: How Scientists Are Moving Beyond Computers to Create a Rival to the Human Brain*. New York: Simon & Schuster, 1994.

Freyd, Jennifer J. *Betrayal Trauma: The Logic of Forgetting Childhood Abuse*. Cambridge, MA: Harvard University Press, 1997.

Gillick, Muriel R. *Tangled Minds: Understanding Alzheimer's Disease and Other Dementias*. New York: Dutton, 1998.

Hacking, Ian. *Rewriting the Soul: Multiple Personality and the Sciences of Memory*. Princeton, NJ: Princeton University Press, 1995.

Hall, Stephen S. "Our Memories, Our Selves," *The New York Times Magazine*, February 15, 1998, 26–57.

Healy, Jane M. *Endangered Minds: Why Children Don't Think and What We Can Do about It*. New York: Simon & Schuster, 1990.

——— . *Failure to Connect: How Computers Affect Our Children's Minds—for Better and Worse*. New York: Simon & Schuster, 1998.

Hilts, Philip J. *Memory's Ghost: The Strange Tale of Mr. M. and the Nature of Memory*. New York: Simon & Schuster, 1995.

Hobson, J. Allan. *The Chemistry of Conscious States: How the Brain Changes Its Mind*. Boston: Little, Brown, 1994.

Jaynes, Julian. *The Origin of Consciousness in the Breakdown of the Bicameral Mind*. Boston: Houghton Mifflin, 1990.

Johnson, George. *In the Palaces of Memory: How We Build the Worlds Inside Our Heads*. New York: Knopf, 1991.

Kotre, John. *White Gloves: How We Create Ourselves Through Memory*. New York: Free Press, 1995.

Kotulak, Ronald. *Inside the Brain: Revolutionary Discoveries of How the Mind Works*. Kansas City MO: Andrews & McMeel, 1997.

Loftus, Elizabeth. *The Myth of Repressed Memory: False Memories and Allegations of Sexual Abuse*. New York: St. Martin's Press, 1994.

Lorayne, Harry, and Jerry Lucas, *The Memory Book*. New York: Ballantine, 1986.

McConkey, James. *The Anatomy of Memory: An Anthology*. New York: Oxford University Press, 1996.

McGowin, Diana Friel. *Living in the Labyrinth: A Personal Journey through the Maze of Alzheimer's*. New York: Delacorte, 1994.

Molloy, William, and Paul Caldwell. *Alzheimer's Disease: Everything You Need to Know*. Buffalo, NY: Firefly Books, 1998.

Nadeau, Robert L. *Minds, Machines, and Human Consciousness: Are There Limits to Artificial Intelligence?* Chicago: Contemporary Books, 1991.

Norretanders, Tor. *The User Illusion: Cutting Consciousness Down to Size*. New York: Viking, 1998.

Ostrander, Sheila, and Lynn Schroeder. *Super-Memory: The Revolution*. Indianapolis, IN: Knowledge Systems, 1998.

Pearsall, Paul. *The Heart's Code*. New York: Broadway, 1998.

Penrose, Roger. *Shadows of the Mind: A Search for the Missing Science of Consciousness*. New York: Oxford University Press, 1996.

Pinker, Steven. *How the Mind Works*. New York: Norton, 1997.

Powell, Douglas H., and Dean K. Whitla. *Profiles in Cognitive Aging*. Cambridge, MA: Harvard University Press, 1994.

Reiser, Morton F. *Memory in Mind and Brain: What Dream Imagery Reveals*. New York: Basic Books, 1990.

Restak, Richard. *The Brain Has a Mind of Its Own: Insights from a Practicing Neurologist*. New York: Crown, 1991.

——— . *The Modular Brain: How New Discoveries in Neuroscience Are Answering Age-Old Questions about Memory, Free Will, Consciousness, and Personal Identity*. New York: Scribner's, 1994.

Robinson, Jill. *Past Forgetting: The True Story of My Memory Lost and Found*. New York: HarperCollins/Cliff, 1999.

Rose, Steven. *The Making of Memory: From Molecules to Mind*. New York: Doubleday, 1994.

Rosenfield, Israel. *The Invention of Memory: A New View of the Brain*. New York: Basic Books, 1988.

——— . *The Strange, Familiar, and Forgotten: An Anatomy of Consciousness*. New York: Random House, 1992.

Rupp, Rebecca. *Committed to Memory: How We Remember and Why We Forget*. New York: Crown, 1998.

Sacks, Oliver W. *The Man Who Mistook His Wife for a Hat*. New York: Summit, 1985.

Sapolsky, Robert. *Stress, the Aging Brain, and the Mechanism of Neuron Death*. Cambridge, MA: MIT Press, 1992.

Schacter, Daniel L. *Searching for Memory: The Brain, the Mind, and the Past*. New York: Basic Books, 1996.

Schank, Roger C. *Tell Me a Story: A New Look at Real and Artificial Memory*. New York: Scribner's, 1990.

Searle, John R. *The Rediscovery of the Mind*. Cambridge, MA: MIT Press, 1992.

Squire, Larry R. *Memory & Brain*. New York: Oxford University Press, 1987.

Terr, Lenore. *Unchained Memories: True Stories of Traumatic Memories*. New York: Basic Books, 1994.

Turkington, Carol. *The Brain Encyclopedia*. New York: Facts on File, 1996.

Wade, Nicholas, ed. *The Science Times Book of the Brain: The Best Science Reporting from the Acclaimed Weekly Section of the New York Times*. New York: Lyons Press, 1998.

Wakefield, Hollida, and Ralph C. Underwager. *Return of the Furies: An Investigation into Recovered Memory Therapy*. Peru, IL: Open Court, 1994.

Weiner, Jonathan. *Time, Love, Memory: A Great Biologist and His Quest for the Origins of Behavior*. New York: Knopf, 1999.

Wright, Robert. *The Moral Animal: Why We Are the Way We Are: The New Science of Evolutionary Psychology.* New York: Random House, 1995.
Yates, Frances A. *The Art of Memory.* London: Pimlico, 1992.

CULTURAL MEMORY

Adler, Mortimer. *The Paideia Proposal: An Educational Manifesto.* New York: Macmillan, 1982.
————. In *Reforming Education: The Opening of the American Mind,* ed. Geraldine Van Doren. New York: Macmillan, 1988.
Allen, Steve. *"Dumbth": And 81 Ways to Make Americans Smarter.* Buffalo, NY: Prometheus, 1991.
Appleby, Joyce; Lynn Hunt; and Margaret Jacob. *Telling the Truth about History.* New York: Norton, 1998.
Atlas, James. *Battle of the Books: The Curriculum Debate in America.* New York: Norton, 1990.
Banks, James A. *An Introduction to Multicultural Education.* Boston: Allyn & Bacon, 1994.
————. *Multiethnic Education: Theory and Practice.* 3d ed. Boston: Allyn & Bacon, 1994.
Bauer, Yehuda, et. al. *Remembering for the Future: Working Papers & Addenda,* Vol. 2, *The Impact of the Holocaust on the Contemporary World.* New York: Pergamon, 1989.
Belz, Herman, et. al. "A Critique of the National History Standards." *Continuity: A Journal of History* (Special Issue), Spring 1995.
Bennett, William J. *The Book of Virtues: A Treasury of the World's Great Moral Stories.* New York: Simon & Schuster, 1993.
————. *The Devaluing of America: The Fight for Our Culture and Our Children.* New York: Summit, 1992.
————. *The Moral Compass.* New York: Simon & Schuster, 1996.
————. *Our Sacred Honor.* New York: Simon & Schuster, 1997.
Ben-Yehuda, Nachman. *The Masada Myth: Collective Memory and Mythmaking in Israel.* Madison: University of Wisconsin Press, 1995.
Bertman, Stephen. *Doorways Through Time: The Romance of Archaeology.* Los Angeles and New York: Jeremy Tarcher/St. Martin's Press, 1986.
————. *Hyperculture: The Human Cost of Speed.* Westport, CT: Praeger, 1998.
Bertonneau, Thomas F. *Declining Standards at Michigan Public Universities.* 2d ed. Midland, MI: Mackinac Center for Public Policy, 1997.
Birkerts, Sven. *The Gutenberg Elegies: The Fate of Reading in an Electronic Age.* New York: Faber & Faber, 1994.
Bloom, Allan. *The Closing of the American Mind.* New York: Simon & Schuster, 1987.

Boyer, Ernest C. *College: The Undergraduate Experience in America*. New York: Harper & Row, 1987.

———. *High School: A Report on Secondary Education in America*. New York: Harper & Row, 1983.

———. *Scholarship Reconsidered: Priorities of the Professoriate*. Princeton, NJ: Carnegie Foundation for the Advancement of Teaching, 1990.

Brear, Holly Beachley. *Inherit the Alamo: Myth and Ritual at an American Shrine*. Austin: University of Texas Press, 1995.

Brokaw, Tom. *The Greatest Generation*. New York: Random House, 1998.

Brown, Harold O. *The Sensate Culture: Reversing America's Decline into Cultural Chaos*. Dallas, TX: Word, 1996.

Carnes, Mark C., ed. *Past Imperfect: History According to the Movies*. New York: Henry Holt, 1995.

Casement, William. *The Great Canon Controversy: The Battle of the Books in Higher Education*. New Brunswick, NJ: Transaction Publishers, 1996.

Collier, James Lincoln. *The Rise of Selfishness in America*. New York: Oxford University Press, 1991.

Cook, Patricia, ed. *Philosophical Imagination and Cultural Memory: Appropriating Historical Traditions*. Durham, NC: Duke University Press, 1993.

Cromer, Alan. *Connected Knowledge: Science, Philosophy, and Education*. New York: Oxford University Press, 1997.

Cummins, Jim, and Dennis Sayers. *Brave New Schools: Challenging Cultural Illiteracy through Global Learning Networks*. New York: St. Martin's Press, 1995.

Delbanco, Andrew. *Required Reading: Why Our American Classics Matter Now*. New York: Farrar, Straus & Giroux, 1997.

Denby, David. *Great Books: My Adventures with Homer, Rousseau, Woolf, and Other Indestructible Writers of the Western World*. New York: Simon & Schuster, 1996.

Donald, Merlin. *Origins of the Modern Mind: Three Stages in the Evolution of Culture and Cognition*. Cambridge, MA: Harvard University Press, 1991.

Edmundson, Mark. "On the Uses of a Liberal Education," *Harper's*, September 1997, 39–49.

Egan, Timothy. *Lasso the Wind: Away to the New West*. New York: Knopf, 1998.

Elliott, Michael. *The Day Before Yesterday: Reconsidering America's Past, Rediscovering the Present*. New York: Simon & Schuster, 1996.

Ellis, John M. *Literature Lost: Social Agendas and the Corruption of the Humanities*. New Haven, CT: Yale University Press, 1997.

Farkas, Steve; Jean Johnson; Will Friedman; and Ali Bers. *Given the Circumstances: Teachers Talk about Public Education Today* (A Report from Public Agenda). New York: Public Agenda, 1996.

Fentress, James, and Chris Wickham. *Social Memory*. Cambridge, MA: Blackwell, 1992.

Finn, Chester E., Jr.; Diane Ravitch; and Robert T. Fancher, eds. *Against Mediocrity: The Humanities in America's High Schools*. New York: Holmes & Meier, 1984.

Florescano, Enrique. *Memory, Myth, and Time in Mexico: From Aztecs to Independence*. Austin: University of Texas Press, 1995.

Foner, Eric. *The Story of American Freedom*. New York: Norton, 1998.

Forché, Carolyn, *Against Forgetting: Twentieth-Century Poetry of Witness*. New York: Norton, 1993.

Fussell, Paul. *Bad: Or, The Dumbing of America*. New York: Summit, 1991.

Gagnon, Paul, and the Bradley Commission on History in the Schools, eds. *Historical Literacy: The Case for History in American Education*. Boston: Houghton Mifflin, 1989.

Gallup Organization, *Geography: An International Survey; Summary of Findings*. Princeton, NJ: Gallup Organization, 1988.

Girling, John. *Myths and Politics in Western Societies: Evaluating Modernity in the United States, Germany, and Great Britain*. New Brunswick, NJ: Transaction Publishers, 1993.

Gitlin, Todd. *The Twilight of Common Dreams: Why America Is Wracked by Culture Wars*. New York: Henry Holt, 1995.

Gress, David. *From Plato to NATO*. New York: Free Press, 1998.

Hadas, Moses. *Humanism: The Greek Ideal and Its Survival*. New York: Harper, 1960.

——— . *Old Wine, New Bottles: A Humanist Teacher at Work*. New York: Pocket Books, 1963.

Hanson, Victor Davis, and John Heath. *Who Killed Homer?* New York: Free Press, 1998.

Hartman, Geoffrey H., ed. *Holocaust Remembrance: The Shapes of Memory*. Cambridge, MA: Blackwell, 1994.

Herf, Jeffrey. *Divided Memory: The Nazi Past in the Two Germanies*. Cambridge, MA: Harvard University Press, 1997.

Herman, Arthur. *The Idea of Decline in Western History*. New York: Free Press, 1997.

Highet, Gilbert. *The Classical Tradition: Greek and Roman Influences on Western Literature*. New York: Oxford University Press, 1957.

Hirsch, E.D. Jr. *Cultural Literacy: What Every American Needs to Know*. Ed. Pat Mulcahy. New York: Random House, 1988.

——— . *First Dictionary of Cultural Literacy: What Our Children Need To Know*. 2d rev. ed. Boston: Houghton Mifflin, 1996.

——— . *The Schools We Need: And Why We Don't Have Them*. New York: Doubleday, 1996.

——— . *What Your Second Grader Needs To Know: The Fundamentals of a Good Second Grade Education*. New York: Dell, 1993.

——— . *What Your Third Grader Needs To Know: The Fundamentals of a Good Third Grade Education*. New York: Dell, 1994.

———. *What Your Fourth Grader Needs To Know: The Fundamentals of a Good Fourth Grade Education*. New York: Dell, 1994.

———. *What Your Fifth Grader Needs To Know: The Fundamentals of a Good Fifth Grade Education*. New York: Dell, 1995.

———. *What Your Sixth Grader Needs To Know: The Fundamentals of a Good Sixth Grade Education*. New York: Dell, 1995.

Hirsch, E. D., and John Holdren. *What Your Kindergartner Needs To Know*. New York: Dell, 1997.

———. *What Your First Grader Needs To Know: The Fundamentals of a Good First Grade Education*. New York: Dell, 1993.

Hirsch, E. D., Jr.; Joseph F. Keh; and James Frejil. *Dictionary of Cultural Literacy*. 2d rev. ed. Boston: Houghton Mifflin, 1993.

Hirsch, Herbert. *Genocide and the Politics of Memory: Studying Death to Preserve Life*. Chapel Hill: University of North Carolina Press, 1995.

Hitchens, Christopher. "Goodbye to All That: Why Americans Are Not Taught History," *Harper's*, November 1998, 37–47.

Hughes, Robert. *The Culture of Complaint: The Fraying of America*. New York: Oxford University Press, 1993.

Humphreys, R. Stephen. *Between Memory and Desire: The Middle East in a Troubled Age*. Berkeley: University of California Press, 1999.

Hunter, James Davison, and Bowman, Carl. *The State of Disunion: 1996 Survey of American Political Culture*. 2 vols. Charlottesville, VA: The Postmodernity Project (University of Virginia), 1996.

Hutchins, Robert Maynard; Mortimer J. Alder; et al., eds. *The Great Books of the Western World*. Chicago: University of Chicago Press/Encyclopedia Britannica, 1952.

Hutton, Patrick H. *History As an Art of Memory*, Hanover, NH: University Press of New England, 1993.

Huyssen, Andreas. *Twilight Memories: Marking Time in a Culture of Amnesia*. New York: Routledge, 1995.

Israeloff, Roberta. *Lost and Found: A Woman Revisits Eighth Grade*. New York: Simon & Schuster, 1996.

Jacoby, Russell. *Social Amnesia: A Critique of Conformist Psychology from Adler to Laing*. Boston: Beacon Press, 1975. (Reissued, with a new foreword by the author, as *Social Amnesia: A Critique of Contemporary Psychology*. New Brunswick, NJ: Transaction Publishers, 1996).

Jameson, Frederic. *Postmodernism or the Cultural Logic of Late Capitalism*. Durham, NC: Duke University Press, 1991.

Johnson, Jean; Steve Farkas; and Ali Bers. *Getting By: What American Teenagers Really Think About Their Schools* (A Report from Public Agenda). New York: Public Agenda, 1997.

Kaplan, Robert D. *An Empire Wilderness: Travels into America's Future*. New York: Random House, 1998.

Kaser, James A. *At the Bivouac of Memory: History, Politics, and the Battle of Chickamauga*. American University Studies, Series 9, "History," Vol. 179. New York: Peter Lang, 1996.

Katz, Jon. *Virtuous Reality: How America Surrendered Discussion of Moral Values to Opportunists, Nitwits and Blockheads like William Bennett*. New York: Random House, 1997.

Kernan, Alvin B. *The Death of Literature*. New Haven, CT: Yale University Press, 1990.

———. *Generation of Change: The Humanities in a Time of Transition*. Princeton, NJ: Princeton University Press, 1997.

———. *In Plato's Cave*. New Haven, CT: Yale University Press, 1999.

Kernan, Alvin B., ed. *What's Happened to the Humanities*. Princeton, NJ: Princeton University Press, 1997.

Knox, Bernard. *Backing into the Future: The Classical Tradition and its Future* . New York: Norton, 1994.

———. *The Oldest Dead White European Males: And Other Reflections on the Classics*. New York: Norton, 1993.

Kolodny, Annette. *Failing the Future: A Dean Looks at Higher Education in the Twenty-first Century*. Durham, NC: Duke University Press, 1998.

Kozol, Jonathan. *Illiterate America*. New York: NAL Dutton, 1986.

Kramer, Hilton, and Roger Kimball. *The Future of the European Past*. Chicago: Ivan R. Dee, 1997.

Kramer, Rita. *Ed School Follies*. New York: Free Press, 1991.

Krauss, Michael I.; Robert Lerner; Althea K. Nagai; and Rita Zurcher. *The Troubling State of General Education: A Study of Six Virginia Public Colleges and Universities*. Rev. ed. Princeton, NJ: National Association of Scholars, 1998.

Kurzweil, Edith, et al., eds. "Education and Integration: Europe and America" (Special Issue with contributions by Nathan Glazer, Rita Kramer, and others), *The Partisan Review*, Summer 1998.

Ladd, Brian. *The Ghosts of Berlin: Confronting German History in the Urban Landscape*. Chicago: University of Chicago Press, 1997.

Landauer, Thomas K. *The Trouble with Computers: Usefulness, Usability, & Productivity*. Cambridge, MA: MIT Press, 1995.

Langer, Lawrence L. *Admitting the Holocaust: Collected Essays*. New York: Oxford, 1995.

———. *Art from the Ashes: A Holocaust Anthology*. New York: Oxford, 1995.

———. *Holocaust Testimonies: The Ruins of Memory*. New Haven, CT: Yale University Press, 1991.

Lanham, Richard A. *Literacy and the Survival of Humanism*. New Haven, CT: Yale University Press, 1983.

Leo, John. *Two Steps Ahead of the Thought Police*. New York: Simon & Schuster, 1994; New Brunswick, NJ: Transaction Publishers, 1998.

Levine, Lawrence W. *The Opening of the American Mind: Canons, Culture, and History*. Boston: Beacon Press, 1996.

Likona, Thomas. *Educating for Character: How Our Schools Can Teach Respect and Responsibility*. New York: Bantam, 1991.

Lipsitz, George. *Time Passages: Collective Memory and American Popular Culture*. Minneapolis: University of Minnesota Press, 1990.

Lipstadt, Deborah E. *Denying the Holocaust: The Growing Assault on Truth and Memory*. New York: Free Press, 1993.

Livingston, James D. "100 Years of Magnetic Memories" in *Scientific American*, November 1998, 106–111.

Loewen, James W. *Lies My Teacher Told Me: Everything Your American History Textbook Got Wrong*. New York: Simon & Schuster, 1996.

Maier, Pauline. *American Scripture: Making the Declaration of Independence*. New York: Knopf, 1997.

Manguel, Alberto. *A History of Reading*. New York: Viking Penguin, 1996.

Marc, David. *Bonfire of the Humanities: Television, Subliteracy, and Long-term Memory Loss*. Syracuse, NY: Syracuse University Press, 1995.

Miller, John J. *The Unmaking of Americans*. New York: Free Press, 1998.

Mitchell, Susan. *The Official Guide to American Attitudes*. Ithaca, NY: American Demographics, 1996.

Nash, Gary B.; Charlotte Crabtree; and Ross E. Dunn. *History on Trial: Culture Wars and the Teaching of the Past*. New York: Knopf, 1997.

National Association of Scholars. *The Dissolution of General Education: 1914–1993*. Princeton, NJ: National Association of Scholars, 1996.

National History Standards Task Force Staff. *National Standards for United States History: Exploring the American Experience*. Los Angeles: National Center for History in the Schools, 1994.

——— . *National Standards for World History: Exploring Paths to the Present*. Los Angeles: National Center for History in the Schools, 1994.

New York Association of Scholars and Empire Foundation for Policy Research. *SUNY's Core Curricula: The Failure to Set Consistent and High Academic Standards*. New York: Empire Foundation for Policy Research, July 1996.

Nussbaum, Martha C. *Cultivating Humanity: A Classical Defense of Reform in Liberal Education*. Cambridge, MA: Harvard University Press, 1998.

Pelikan, Jaroslav J. *The Idea of the University: A Reexamination*. New Haven, CT: Yale University Press, 1992.

Penny, Jocelyn. *Wax Tablets of the Mind: Cognitive Studies of Memory and Literacy in Classical Antiquity* London: Routledge, 1997.

Postman, Neil. *Amusing Ourselves to Death: Public Discourse in the Age of Show Business*. New York: Viking Penguin, 1986.

——— . *The End of Education: Redefining the Value of Schools*. New York: Knopf, 1995.

————. *Technopoly: The Surrender of Culture to Technology.* New York: Random House, 1992.

Postman, Neil, and Charles Weingartner. *Teaching as a Subversive Activity.* New York: Delacorte, 1969.

Proctor, Robert E. *Education's Great Amnesia: Reconsidering the Humanities from Petrarch to Freud with a Curriculum for Today's Students.* Bloomington, IN: Indiana University Press, 1988.

Ravitch, Diane. "Tot Sociology: or What Happened to History in the Grade Schools," *American Scholar* 56 (Summer 1987), 343–354.

Ravitch, Diane and Chester E. Finn, Jr. *What Do Our 17-Year-Olds Know? A Report on the First National Assessment of History and Literature.* New York: Harper & Row, 1987.

Reinhold, Meyer. *Classica Americana: The Greek and Roman Heritage in the United States.* Detroit: Wayne State University Press, 1984.

————. *The Classick Pages: Classical Reading of Eighteenth-Century Americans.* University Park, PA: American Philological Association, 1975.

Reynolds, Donald Martin, ed. *"Remove Not the Ancient Landmark": Public Monuments and Moral Values.* Amsterdam: Gordon & Breach, 1996.

Richard, Carl J. *The Founders and the Classics: Greece, Rome, and the American Enlightenment.* Cambridge, MA: Harvard University Press, 1994.

Rorty, Richard. *Achieving Our Country: Leftist Thought in Twentieth Century America.* Cambridge, MA: Harvard University Press, 1998.

Roszak, Theodore. *America the Wise: The Longevity Revolution and the True Wealth of Nations.* Boston: Houghton Mifflin, 1998.

————. *The Cult of Information: A Neo-Luddite Treatise on High-Tech, Artificial Intelligence, and the True Art of Thinking.* Berkeley and Los Angeles: University of California Press, 1994.

Sanders, Barry. *A Is for Ox: Violence, Electronic Media, and the Silencing of the Written Word.* New York: Random House, 1995.

Saul, John Ralston. *The Unconscious Civilization.* Toronto: House of Anansi Press, 1995.

Schama, Simon. *Landscape and Memory.* New York: Knopf, 1995.

Schleifer, R.; R. C. Davis; and N. Mergler. *Culture and Cognition: the Boundaries of Literary and Scientific Thought.* Ithaca, NY: Cornell University Press, 1992.

Schlesinger, Arthur M., Jr. *The Disuniting of America: Reflections on a Multicultural Society.* Knoxville, TN: Whittle Direct Books, 1991.

Schmandt-Besserat, Denise. *Before Writing.* 2 vols. Austin: University of Texas Press, 1992.

————. *How Writing Came About.* Austin: University of Texas Press, 1997.

Schmidt, Michael. *The New Reich: Violent Extremism in Unified Germany and Beyond.* New York: Pantheon, 1993.

Seelye, John. *Memory's Nation: The Place of Plymouth Rock*. Chapel Hill: University of North Carolina Press, 1998.

Sewall, Gilbert T. "The Postmodern Schoolhouse." In Katherine Washborn and John Thornton, eds., *Dumbing Down: Essays on the Strip-Mining of American Culture*. New York: Norton, 1997, 57–67.

Shenkman, Richard. *Legends and Lies in World History*. New York: HarperCollins, 1994.

Silberman, Neil Asher. *Between Past and Present: Archaeology, Ideology, and Nationalism in the Modern Middle East*. New York: Henry Holt, 1989.

Shrimpton, Gordon S. *History and Memory in Ancient Greece*. Montreal, Quebec, and Kingston, Ontario: McGill-Queen's University Press, 1997.

Sizer, Theodore R. *Horace's Compromise: The Dilemma of the American High School*. Boston: Houghton Mifflin, 1984.

———. *Horace's Hope: What Works for the American High School*. Boston: Houghton Mifflin, 1996.

———. *Horace's School*. Rev. ed. Boston: Houghton Mifflin, 1997.

Small, Jocelyn Penny. *Wax Tablets of the Mind: Cognitive Studies of Memory and Literacy in Classical Antiquity*. New York: Routledge, 1997.

Smith, George S., and John E. Ehrenhard. *Protecting the Past*. Boca Raton, FL: CRC Press, 1991.

Smith, Thomas M. *High School Students Ten Years after "A Nation at Risk": Findings from "The Condition of Education, 1994."* Washington, DC: National Center for Educational Statistics, 1995.

Solway, David. *Lying about the Wolf: Essays in Culture and Education*. Montreal, Quebec, and Kingston, Ontario: McGill-Queen's University Press, 1997.

Sousa, Ronald W., and Joel Weinsheimer. *The Humanities in Dispute: A Dialogue in Letters*. West Lafayette, IN: Purdue University Press, 1998.

Sowell, Thomas. *Inside American Education: The Decline, the Deception, the Dogmas*. New York: Free Press, 1993.

Stark, Steven. *Glued to the Set: The 60 Television Shows and Events That Made Us Who We Are Today*. New York: Free Press, 1997.

Steinberg, Laurence. *Beyond the Classroom: Why School Reform Has Failed and What Parents Need to Do*. New York: Simon & Schuster, 1996.

Sticht, Thomas G.; Carolyn Huie Hofstetter; and C. Richard Hofstetter. *Knowledge, Literacy and Life in San Diego*. San Diego, CA: San Diego Consortium for Workforce Education and Lifelong Learning (CWELL), 1995.

Stoll, Clifford. *Silicon Snake Oil: Second Thoughts on the Information Highway*. New York: Doubleday, *1995*.

Stotsky, Sandra. *Losing Our Language*. New York: Free Press, 1999.

Sturken, Marita. *Tangled Memories: The Vietnam War, the AIDS Epidemic, and the Politics of Remembering*. Berkeley, CA: University of California Press, 1997.

Sugden, John. *Tecumseh: A Life*. New York: Henry Holt, 1998.

Sykes, Charles J. *Dumbing Down Our Kids: Why American Children Feel Good about Themselves but Can't Read, Write, or Add*. New York: St. Martin's Press, 1995.

———. *ProfScam* New York: Regnery, 1988.

Taylor, Gary. *Cultural Selection: Why Some Achievements Survive the Test of Time and Others Don't*. New York: Basic Books, 1996.

Toffler, Alvin. *Future Shock*. New York: Random House, 1970.

Trouillot, Michel-Rolph. *Silencing the Past: Power and the Production of History*. Boston: Beacon Press, 1995.

Turner, Frederick. *The Culture of Hope: A New Birth of the Classical Spirit*. New York: Free Press, 1995.

———. "The Freedoms of the Past: On the Advantage of Looking Backward" *Harper's*, April 1995, 59–62.

United States National Commission on Excellence in Education. *A Nation at Risk: The Imperative for Educational Reform*. Washington, DC: U.S. Government Printing Office, 1983.

Vidal-Naquet, Pierre. *Assassins of Memory: Essays on the Denial of the Holocaust*. New York: Columbia University Press, 1993.

Ward, F. Champion, ed. *The Idea and Practice of General Education*. Chicago: University of Chicago Press, 1993 (1950).

Washburn, Katharine, and John Thornton, eds. *Dumbing Down: Essays on the Strip-Mining of American Culture*. New York: Norton, 1996.

Welsh, Patrick. "Our Teens Are Becoming Lookworms—Instead of Bookworms." *TV Guide*, May 23, 1987, 3ff.

Wiesel, Eli. *The Forgotten*. New York: Summit, 1992.

Wildavsky, Aaron. *The Rise of Radical Egalitarianism*. Washington, DC: American University Press, 1991.

Wills, Garry. *John Wayne's America: The Politics of Celebrity*. New York: Simon & Schuster, 1997.

Wiltshire, Susan Ford. *Greece, Rome, and the Bill of Rights*. Norman: University of Oklahoma Press, 1992.

Windschuttle, Keith. *The Killing of History: How a Discipline Is Being Murdered by Literary Critics and Social Theorists*. Sydney, Australia: MaCleay Press, 1996; New York: Free Press, 1997.

Yates, Frances A. *The Art of Memory*. London: Pimlico, 1966.

Young, James E. *The Texture of Memory: Holocaust Memorials and Meaning*. New Haven, CT: Yale University Press, 1993.

INDEX

About the Author

STEPHEN BERTMAN is Professor of Languages, Literatures, and Cultures at Canada's University of Windsor. He is the author of *Hyperculture: The Human Cost of Speed* (Praeger, 1998).